CW01506475

Contents

Acronyms

A&AEE	Aeroplane & Armament Experimental Establishment
ACMI	Air Combat Manoeuvering Instrumentation
ADS	Air Director School
ADTU	Air Director Training Unit
AFC	Air Force Cross
AFDS	Air Fighting Development School
AIM	Air Interception Missile
AOC	Air Officer Commanding
ATAC	Army Tactical Missile
AWA	Armstrong Whitworth Aircraft
BBMF	Battle of Britain Memorial Flight
CA	Controller Aircraft
CAA	Civil Aviation Authority
CAP	Combat Air Patrols
CAW	College of Air Warfare
CFE	Central Fighter Establishment
CFS	Central Flying School
CO	Commanding Officer
CofA	Certificate of Airworthiness
COMA	Civil-Owned Military Aircraft
DFC	Distinguished Flying Cross
DFCS	Day Fighter Combat Squadron
DFLS	Day Fighter Leader School
DRA	Defense Research Association
DSO	Distinguished Service Order
ETPS	Empire Test Pilots' School
EW	Electronic Warfare
FAA	Fleet Air Arm
FAST	Farnborough Air Sciences Trust
FONAC	Flag Officer Naval Air Command

HAWKER
HUNTER

HAWKER HUNTER

A CLASSIC BRITISH JET FIGHTER

PHILIP BIRTLES

FONTHILL

Fonthill Media Language Policy

Fonthill Media publishes in the international English language market. One language edition is published worldwide. As there are minor differences in spelling and presentation, especially with regard to American English and British English, a policy is necessary to define which form of English to use. The Fonthill Policy is to use the form of English native to the author. Philip Birtles was born in Edgware, educated in Croydon, and now lives at Stevenage, therefore British English has been adopted in this publication.

www.fonthill.media
office@fonthillmedia.com

First published in the United Kingdom
and the United States of America 2023

British Library Cataloguing in Publication Data:
A catalogue record for this book is available from the British Library

Copyright © Philip Birtles 2023

ISBN 978-1-78155-893-5

Typeset in 10.5pt on 13pt Sabon
Printed and bound in England

FONFT	Flag Officer Naval Flying Training
FRADU	Fleet Requirements and Air Director Unit
FRU	Fleet Requirements Unit
FTS	Flying Training School
FWS	Fighter Weapons School
GCI	Ground Control Interception
HAL	Hawker Aircraft Limited
HHA	Hawker Hunter Aviation
HSA	Hawker Siddeley Aviation
HUD	Head-Up Display
IFIS	Integrated Flight Instrument System
IRS	Infrared System
ITP	Instruction to Proceed
LFC	Lightning Flying Club
MEAF	Middle East Air Force
MOD	Ministry of Defence
MOS	Ministry of Supply
MU	Maintenance Unit
NAFS	Naval Air Fighter School
NAS	Naval Air Squadron
NATO	North Atlantic Treaty Organisation
OCU	Operational Conversion Unit
OFMC	Old Flying Machine Company
OSP	Offshore Procurement Bill
OTU	Operational Training Unit
QFI	Qualified Flying Instructor
RAAF	Royal Australian Air Force
RAE	Royal Aircraft Establishment
RAFA	Royal Air Force Association
RATOG	Rocket-Assisted Take-Off Gear
RAuxAF	Royal Auxiliary Air Force
RhAF	Rhodesian Air Force
ROC	Royal Observer Corps
RP	Rocket Projectiles
RRAF	Royal Rhodesian Air Force
RSAF	Royal Saudi Air Force
RWR	Radar Warning Receivers
SAH	School of Aircraft Handling
SBAC	Society of British Aircraft Companies
SNEB	Société Nouvelle des Etablissements Edgar Brandt
SofTT	School of Technical Training
SRAAM	Short-Range Air-to-Air Missile
TACAN	Tactical Air Navigation System
TAF	Tactical Air Force

TWU	Tactical Weapons Unit
UDI	Unilateral Declaration of Independence
ZAF	Zimbabwe Air Force

Introduction

My first memory of the Hawker Hunter was at the annual Farnborough Air Show in September 1953, where the aircraft was demonstrated by Neville Duke, the Hawker chief test pilot. The commentary was by Major Oliver Stewart, First World War flying ace and editor of *Aeronautics*, with the orientation of the black sheds to the right and Laffan's Plain at the left-hand end. Neville Duke's demonstration included showing off the full capability of the aircraft, including a sonic boom from a dive from high altitude. The test pilots then were almost household names: John Cunningham was demonstrating the Comet, Roland Beaumont the Canberra, Mike Lithgow the Supermarine Swift. I returned to Farnborough in 1954 and 1955 carrying my box Brownie camera and took a picture of the Hunter in the static park among the other types. My enthusiasm for aviation was awakened and I have attended the Farnborough Air Shows ever since, although they are no longer held annually and no longer showcase only aircraft of British design and development, powered by British engines.

When the Hunters entered service with the RAF they had a very short endurance: I remember one making an emergency landing on the short cross runway at Kenley, overshooting and stopping with its nose hanging over Old Lodge Lane. Hunters were also operating with 41 Squadron at Biggin Hill, where I used to go on my bike, pushing up the hill to the Salt Box. It was such a sleek and purposeful aircraft—the classic jet fighter—and the twenty-two Hunters of the 111 Squadron 'Black Arrows' led by Squadron Leader Roger Topp were an astonishing spectacle.

Having chosen an industry career instead of joining the RAF, I was accepted into the de Havilland Aeronautical School at Hatfield where my interest in aviation expanded, but my special interest in the Hunter never left me. I continued to attend air displays, including the annual Battle of Britain shows, particularly at Biggin Hill and further afield, and followed Hunter developments through to the highly effective FGA.9 ground-attack version, which operated with 1 and 54 Squadrons based at West Raynham. I also got a chance to ride in a Hunter T.8B (WV322) from Honington, which served with 237 OCU, supporting the entry

Hunter FR.4 WT780 in the Farnborough static park in September 1955. (*Philip Birtles*)

Hunter F.5 WP186 PT of 41 Squadron on finals to land at Biggin Hill in April 1957. (*Philip Birtles*)

into service of Buccaneer S.2s with 12 Squadron. I was airborne for one hour five minutes on an air-to-air sortie of a formation of Buccaneers with 237 OCU, 12 Squadron and 809 Naval Air Squadron (NAS). Having been provided with lunch before the flight, I have a memory of being airsick into the pilot's leather glove, as there were no sick bags. We flew at very low level over the North Sea and I have a sideways-blurred picture of a ferry as we flew over.

With the start of the new millennium there was a growing enthusiasm for the Hunter as a privately owned and operated warbird. Although not cheap to operate, it was affordable for some and popular at air shows, and the availability of flying two-seat Hunters, with plentiful spares, made conversion practical. The centre for these activities was the aviation company Delta Jets, based at the former RAF Kemble 5 Maintenance Unit (MU) airfield. While a number of Hunters found their way into aviation museums, a number of low-hour good-condition candidates were restored to flying condition and qualified for a certificate of airworthiness (CofA). Hunters were not only flying in Britain, but also in Europe; but all this stopped on 22 August 2015 with the crash of T.7 WV372 at Shoreham. The CofA was withdrawn and all Hunter flying ceased, except for that of a pair of ex-Swiss Hunter F.58s. These planes are operated on the military register by Hawker Hunter Aviation, based at Scampton, and are used on military contracts.

Hunter T.8B WV322 of 237 OCU at Honington, August 1973. (*Philip Birtles*)

1

Hawker Jet Fighter Development

As the Second World War began its final phase, the RAF had a highly developed range of combat aircraft mainly powered by traditional piston engines. This concept had reached its ultimate capability with some airframes experiencing compressibility as they neared the speed of sound. Although at a slow rate, work had fortunately progressed during the Second World War on turbojet development, led by Frank Whittle. The turbojet briefly entered service with 616 Squadron as the powerplant for early Gloster Meteors, the only allied jet to serve in the war, but the Germans were far ahead: they had already developed practical jet engines and used them in combat. After the war, British engineers were able to access German technology in both engines and airframes.

In March 1938, before the outbreak of war, when the potential for the new power source was beginning to be realised, the Air Ministry placed a contract with Frank Whittle's company, Power Jets, to design, develop and construct a turbojet engine to flight standard. But it was not until February 1940 that the government fully backed the concept by placing an order for a suitable airframe to meet Specification E.28/39 with the Gloster Aircraft Company. By this time Germany had already test flown a jet engine and were developing an operational jet fighter. The Air Ministry's specification called for only a simple airframe designed as a test bed for the new engine, but the airframe was also to be capable of being developed into a fighter with fixed guns. The low power, however, would have made combat impractical.

Britain at the time was engaged in a desperate battle of survival against Nazi Germany, and the government was more concerned with the production of traditional combat aircraft for immediate use than expending limited resources on a new, untried concept. However, spurred on by intelligence of German developments, the Air Ministry issued Specification F.9/40 to cover a Gloster proposal for a twin 2,000-lb-thrust jet fighter armed with six fixed 20-mm cannons. The development of early jet engines progressed, and an order was placed for twelve of the Gloster aircraft in February 1941. Meanwhile, in April 1941, the E.28/39, by now named Pioneer, made a few hops from the restricted Gloster airfield at Hucclecote. The first successful flight was from the more suitably remote airfield at Cranwell on

15 May 1941, with Gerry Sayer as pilot. Although the Pioneer did not have a sparkling performance, it did prove that the concept of a jet engine was practical.

The production of jet engines in any quantity required special manufacturing facilities using new materials at high temperatures. Investment in jet engine development was very low at the time, but Rover took an early lead, and the Rover W.2B was chosen as the powerplant for the new Gloster fighter. It was, however, only capable of producing 1,000 lb of thrust, which was totally inadequate for the new fighter. Fortunately Major Frank Halford of the de Havilland Engine Company was also working on jet engine development with the full backing of a major industrial organisation. The company developed the H.1, which produced 1,500 lb of thrust. Two of these jet engines were sufficiently powerful to allow the first F.9/40 fighter to make a successful maiden flight on 5 March 1943. The Halford H.1 was later developed into the Goblin, which powered the de Havilland Vampire jet fighter which first flew from Hatfield on 29 September 1943. The Goblin was the first jet engine to go into series production.

The early jet engines were not only low on power, but aircraft endurance was very limited. Meanwhile, Rolls-Royce took over development of the W.2B, resulting in the Welland, which boasted 1,700 lb of thrust. This engine powered the production version of the Gloster fighter, named the Meteor F.1. Meteor F.1s entered service with 616 Squadron based at RAF Manston towards the end of the war, but the Vampire arrived too late to take an active part in the Second World War. Although both the Meteor and Vampire had little performance improvement over existing combat aircraft, they demonstrated the potential for an overall improvement in performance well beyond existing capabilities.

In the autumn of 1944, with the end of the Second World War in sight and production lines busy with Typhoons and Tempests, Hawker Aircraft began to look at the concept of a jet fighter. With preliminary details of the Rolls-Royce B.41 turbojet (later named the Nene) made available, the Hawker design team, led by Sydney Camm, incorporated the engine in the centre fuselage of the F.2/43 Fury in November 1944. This became P1035. The jet engine was mounted on the centre of gravity with air intakes in the wing roots and exhaust at the tail. The concept was further refined as P1040 the following month, with air intakes in the roots of the straight wing, and bifurcated jet pipes exhausting on either side of the fuselage behind the wing trailing edge. With the low efficiency of early jet engines, the shorter jet pipes gave the best available power. At this time, jet power was beginning to show an improvement over the traditional piston-engine-driven propeller.

Early in the new year of 1945, the air staff approved the general design, allowing Hawker to proceed with detailed design, working with Rolls-Royce on powerplant installation, but despite a tender being submitted in February, there was a delay of many months before a specification was issued. This was due to the aircraft's unorthodox design. Both the air staff and Admiralty continued to maintain an interest, while the development of intakes, engines and jet-pipe configurations was studied. By October 1945 there was sufficient data available for Hawker to issue a production order to start building a prototype.

At this point the air staff interest reduced: they did not credit the aircraft with a sufficient improvement in performance over the Gloster Meteor IV, which had established a new world speed record of 606 mph. However, the Admiralty recognised the potential of P1040 as a fleet support fighter superior to the Supermarine Attacker then entering service. The Hawker aircraft was therefore tendered in January 1946 as a carrier-based interceptor. Specification N.7/46 was issued with an 'instruction to proceed' on the construction of three flying prototypes and a test specimen. This was covered by a contract in May 1946, which specified that the first aircraft would be an aerodynamic prototype without armament or operational equipment.

The prototype P1040 VP401 was flown for the first time from the Aeroplane & Armament Experimental Establishment (A&AEE) at Boscombe Down on 2 September 1947 by the Hawker chief test pilot, Squadron Leader Trevor 'Wimpy' Wade. It was transferred to the Royal Aircraft Establishment (RAE) at Farnborough three days later.

P1040 VP401 was a traditional all-metal design with mid-mounted wings attached to stub roots integral with the fuselage, incorporating the engine air intakes. The pilot was located under a bubble canopy with manual controls in the forward fuselage and an excellent all-round view. The tailplane was mounted halfway up the single fin. The engine was initially a 4,500-lb-thrust Rolls-Royce Nene I turbojet, situated

P.1040 prototype VP401, which was flown from Boscombe Down on 2 September 1947 as Hawker's first jet aircraft. (*BAE Systems*)

in the centre fuselage on the centre of gravity. This was later replaced by a 5,000-lb-thrust Nene II. The Nene was a centrifugal turbojet that used proven technology but was not particularly efficient. The straight wings had a thickness/chord ratio of 0.095, with fuel tanks of 395-gallon capacity in the fuselage forward and aft of the engine, giving an endurance of over two hours. Additional drop fuel tanks with a capacity of 90 gallons each could be carried on underwing pylons.

The first fully equipped naval N.7/46 prototype VP413 had its maiden flight on 3 September 1948. It featured folding wings, arrester hook and catapult spools. The under forward fuselage gun armament consisted of four fixed 20-mm Hispano cannons with 200 rounds per gun. In April 1949, following initial dummy-deck assessment trials at Boscombe Down, VP413 was flown on HMS *Illustrious* for full-deck trials, including landing, take-off and general handling operations. In July the wingspan was increased by 30 inches, ready for a full programme of service and evaluation trials. In September, during the trials, it made its first public appearance at the Farnborough Air Show.

P1040, meanwhile, took part in the National Air Races on 1 August 1949. Flown by Wimpy Wade, it achieved an average speed on 510 mph in the SBAC Challenge Cup at Elmdon. The aircraft was then returned to Kingston to have an Armstrong Siddeley Snarler rocket engine installed in the rear fuselage. It was then redesignated P1072.

The final flying prototype P1040 VP422 flew for the first time on 17 October 1949 and differed from the previous prototype in having provision for rocket-assisted take-off gear (RATOG). This aircraft was used for further deck trials in February 1950, followed by gun-firing and drop-tank-carrying trials. These two aircraft went on to participate in more advanced service trials including catapult take-offs, hood jettisoning and various air brake installations.

By this time an order for 151 production Sea Hawk F.1s had been placed, while WF143, the first production aircraft powered by a Nene 101 engine, was flown on 14 November 1951. When problems were found with lateral control, power-assisted ailerons were introduced for the fifth production aircraft, WF145, which became the prototype Mk 2. A number of the early production aircraft were used for service and operational trials, ready for the first operational F.1s to be introduced to 806 NAS (Naval Air Squadron) at Brawdy in south Wales in March 1953. Further aircraft were scheduled to equip both 804 and 898 NAS.

With the government's introduction of the 'super priority' production programme, there was insufficient manufacturing capacity at Kingston and Langley for both the Sea Hawk and, later, the Hunter. This resulted in Sea Hawk production being transferred to Armstrong Whitworth Aircraft (AWA), a member company of the Hawker Siddeley Group, at Coventry. Only thirty-five F.1s were produced by Hawker before the transfer to Coventry, while the first AWA aircraft, F.1 WF162, was flying before the end of 1953. With the completion of sixty F.1s, AWA production was transferred to the F.2s with full-powered ailerons. Forty had been built by early 1954, and these replaced the F.1s of 806 NAS. Both the early marks were capable of carrying 90-gallon drop tanks. The FB.3 was introduced

The first production Sea Hawk F.1, WF143, which was first flown on 14 November 1951. (*BAE Systems*)

as a fighter bomber with 116 built at Coventry during 1954. These aircraft were capable of carrying two 500-lb bombs or mines in place of the fuel drop tanks. The first one, WF280, flew from Baginton on 13 March 1954. This version equipped 800, 801, 806, 897 and 898 NAS.

The next major development was the FGA.4 ground-attack fighter. The first, WV792, flew on 26 August 1954. It featured additional wing strong points, which included the carriage of up to twenty 3-inch rocket projectiles (RP) with 60-lb warheads. A total of ninety-seven FGA.4s were built by AWA, with deliveries to the Fleet Air Arm (FAA) from the end of the year. To improve on the relatively low performance of the FB.3 and FGA.4, the more powerful 5,200-lb-thrust Nene 103 was installed. This modification gave birth to the Sea Hawk Mk 5 and 6, and eighty-six new-build FGA.6s were also ordered. Sea Hawks were used operationally in the Suez campaign in November 1956, flown by 800, 802, 804, 897 and 899 NAS, covering the Anglo-French landings in Egypt and operating ground attacks against Egyptian airfields. Supermarine Scimitars began to replace Sea Hawks in 1958, although Sea Hawks remained in front-line strength until 1960.

In addition to a small number of ex-FAA Sea Hawks supplied to the Royal Australian Navy, there were three export orders. In 1956, some months after the FAA production had ceased, the West German Navy ordered thirty-two Mk 100 day fighters and thirty-two Mk 101 single-seat all-weather fighters. The Ekco AI radar was mounted in a pod under the starboard wing, and to balance the additional side aerodynamic loads, fin and rudder areas were increased. At the same time the Netherlands ordered thirty-two Mk 50 Sea Hawks which were similar to the FGA.6s,

Sea Hawk F.1s with 806 NAS at Brawdy, demonstrating their folding wings. (*BAE Systems*)

Sea Hawk FGA.4 XE443 at the Farnborough Air Show in September 1955, promoting export sales. (*Philip Birtles*)

but equipped with UHF radio. These orders made reopening the production line worthwhile. The final export order was in September 1959 with fourteen FGA.6s for the Indian Air Force. The aircraft were delivered in 1960.

In October 1945, with construction of the P1040 about to start, Hawker Aircraft submitted a design study for the P1040 to be fitted with swept-back wings. The aircraft was to have the designation P1047 and be powered by a rocket engine. The project was of interest to the RAE at Farnborough. Specification N.7/46 was also to include a swept-wing research aircraft based on the Hawker proposal. Rocket power was not adopted immediately, although it was later tested in the P1072. As a result of continuing discussions with the Air Ministry and Ministry of Supply, a new specification, E.38/46, was issued for the study of the aerodynamics of swept wings, and a production order was authorised for the construction of a prototype P1052. The specification was received by Hawker on 16 January 1947; in March Hawker submitted their tender, which was accepted, authorising the construction of two prototypes: VX272 and VX279.

Powered by a 5,000-lb-thrust Rolls-Royce Nene RN.2, the P1052s were similar to the P1040 except for their 35-degree swept-back wings with a thickness/chord ratio of 0.10. Although a swept-back tailplane had been considered, it remained straight as with the earlier aircraft. It was anticipated the swept-back wings would investigate flight data for speeds of up to Mach 0.86, with a top speed of 560 mph at 36,000 feet. In October 1948, the P1052's advance in performance over the Gloster Meteor resulted in a proposal to put the type into quantity production. However, this was subsequently rejected as a number of advanced designs were already being considered for the future.

The first prototype was constructed in the experimental shop at the newly acquired Richmond Road factory in November 1948. On 19 November it was moved to Boscombe Down for the first flight by Wimpy Wade. The second prototype, VX279, joined the flight test programme on 13 April 1949, and both aircraft demonstrated an increased performance over the predicted figures. In June, VX272 was delivered to the RAE at Farnborough. Meanwhile, VX279 went to the A&AEE at Boscombe Down for assessment as a possible future fighter for the RAAF, with the proposal that it would be powered by a reheat version of the Nene, known as the Tay, and have a swept-back tailplane and straight-through exhaust.

On 29 September 1949, VX272 suffered a forced landing. During repairs, a variable incidence tailplane was incorporated. This was completed by March 1950, and the following month, VX279 was returned to Kingston for conversion to the P1081. The rear fuselage of VX279 was removed and strengthened for fitting with an arrester hook for deck-landing trials later in the year. Unfortunately VX279 was damaged seriously in a crash landing and further repairs were not completed until September 1951, when on its first flight after the repairs it suffered another forced landing, although with less damage.

In March 1952 VX272 was used for a series of high-speed trials with a large bullet fairing fitted to the fin/tailplane intersection giving improved high Mach

German Navy Sea Hawk Mk 100s at Bitteswell. Included among them is VA222. (*BAE Systems*)

The second P.1052 prototype, VX279, powered by a Rolls-Royce Nene turbojet with swept-back wings and straight tail. (*BAE Systems*)

number characteristics. During May 1952 deck trials were finally carried out aboard HMS *Eagle,* but by then the requirement had reduced. The aircraft then went again to the RAE at Farnborough for further high-speed trials, until in September 1953 it suffered its final forced landing. It was superficially repaired and allocated to ground instruction as 7174M at RAF Halton before becoming gate guard at RAF Cardington for a while. It was saved for preservation by the RAF Colerne Museum and is now stored in the reserve collection of the Fleet Air Arm Museum at Yeovilton.

When the original rocket-powered P1040 proposal was made in October 1945, there were no rockets existing in Britain. Towards the end of 1947 further interest in a rocket installation was aroused with Armstrong Siddeley Motors starting work on a 2,000-lb-thrust rocket. Although consideration was given to building another P1040, by the time the rocket was ready VP401 had completed its flight development contribution to N.7/46 and was converted to rocket power from September 1949 as the P1072.

The conversion required some fairly substantial internal modifications due to the use of methanol-water and liquid oxygen fuel. This fuel had to be stored internally, which reduced the capacity of turbojet fuel to 175 gallons. In the forward fuselage, 75 gallons of liquid oxygen were carried in a spherical tank, while aft of the jet fuel tank was a 120-gallon water-methanol tank. The Armstrong Siddeley Snarler rocket motor was mounted in the extreme tail under the rudder. A separate pneumatic system operated the rocket fuel controls, and the liquid oxygen supply pipe was located under the centre fuselage.

The Snarler and its associated equipment was delivered from Anstey to Kingston in June 1950 for installation in VP401, and on 16 November VP401 was flown to Bitteswell, the Armstrong Whitworth test airfield, on Nene power only. On 20 November the rocket was ignited and expended its full load of fuel, but due to the Air Ministry favouring the more practical reheat turbojets, this was one of only half a dozen flights made using rocket power. During the last flight there was a minor explosion in the engine causing slight damage, and although it was repaired the aircraft never flew again.

With continuing interest from Australia, Hawker proposed replacing the Nene engine in P1052 VX279 with a Rolls-Royce Tay. Delays with the Tay, however, resulted in the 5,000-lb-thrust Nene being retained, although the rear fuselage was replaced with a straight-through jet-pipe exhaust from the rear fuselage and fitted with swept-back tail surfaces. The aircraft was designated P1081 and was first flown by Wimpy Wade on 19 June 1950. Flight trials continued throughout the year on various refinements, but on 14 November Hawker was notified that work was to stop on the Australian project. Two months later the aircraft was delivered to the RAE at Farnborough for further research flying, but on 3 April 1951, when flying P1081, Wimpy Wade was killed in an unexplained crash having attempted to eject at too low an altitude.

The first P.1052 prototype, VX272, when in the care of RAF Colerne Museum, July 1975. (*Philip Birtles*)

P.1072 VP401 fitted with an Armstrong Siddeley Snarler rocket in the rear fuselage. (*BAE Systems*)

P.1072 VP401 with a Snarler rocket-assisted take-off. (*BAE Systems*)

P.1081 VX279 powered by a Rolls-Royce Nene with straight-through jet pipe exhausting from the rear fuselage and swept-back aerofoils. This aircraft was lost on 3 April 1951, killing Wimpy Wade. (*BAE Systems*)

2

Hunter Design and Development

With the two specifications issued in 1946 failing to produce a Gloster Meteor replacement, Hawker began project design of a day fighter powered by the more efficient Rolls-Royce AJ.65 axial flow turbojet, later named Avon, with an expected thrust of 6,500 lb. This new turbojet would be a much smaller diameter, reducing drag. Preliminary work continued during 1947, and in January 1948, before an official requirement was defined, Hawker offered the new design, the P1067, to the Air Ministry. The configuration of the new design, with sweep back on all surfaces and a tailplane on top of the fin, had a pilot in the front fuselage with an engine air intake in the extreme nose. The proposed armament consisted of two newly designed 30-mm Aden cannons. In March 1948 a new specification, F.3/48, was issued, and Hawker was invited to offer their P1067. Development of the Avon engine proved to be more demanding than expected, taking some seven years. The main challenge was moving from the tried and tested, but less efficient, centrifugal configuration to the straight-through axial layout. The similar Armstrong Whitworth Sapphire, developed from the Metrovick F9 of Second World War vintage, was a more mature, lower cost design with greater reliability, but Sydney Camm, head of the Hawker design team, had a strong loyalty to Rolls-Royce and the Avon, and continued to specify it for P1067.

The new specification called for a single-seat land-based day fighter capable of achieving Mach 0.94, which was equivalent to 620 mph at 36,000 feet, or 724 mph at sea level. The aircraft was to be capable of intercepting high-altitude bombers, then under development in the Soviet Union. A radar-ranging gunsight was fitted in the nose, and the pilot was to sit in an ejection seat for emergency abandonment at high speed and altitude. Required fuel endurance was for sixty minutes. Operational Requirement 228/3 was issued to cover the project, and as an insurance against development difficulties with either turbojet, power was to come from either Avon or Sapphire engines. The OR called for a time to height of less than six minutes from engine start to 45,000 feet, giving time for the aircraft to intercept an incoming hostile bomber from a safe distance after identification by ground-based radars. Up to 50,000 feet, a climb rate of 1,000 feet per minute was expected. To ensure compatibility with RAF airfields, a take-off distance of 1,200 yards was specified; however, to achieve greater levels of safety, runways at many fighter stations were extended.

Hawker's initial design configuration started with a T-tail and twin underwing air intakes on a flattened elliptical fuselage, which gradually evolved, with the intake being moved to the nose position and the fuselage becoming a traditional circular cross-section. The four nose-mounted cannons were reduced to one in each wing root, but there was still concern that there would be insufficient room for the nose-mounted radar-ranging system. There were also concerns from Rolls-Royce that the efficiency of the Avon could be reduced by a long air intake ducting. Although Camm and his team were reluctant to change the intake position again, it soon became obvious that wing-root intakes were a better option as they allowed space for fuel capacity in the forward fuselage and created more room in the cockpit. Therefore, wing-root intakes were preferred.

Detail design started in May 1948 with contract cover provided a month later, calling for the manufacture of three prototypes, one of which was to be powered by an Armstrong Siddeley Sapphire turbojet, and the other two by the Rolls-Royce Avon. Following preliminary wind-tunnel tests, the tailplane was lowered on the fin and the engine air intakes were moved to the wing roots to allow for the installation of a radar-ranging system in the nose. Armament was increased from two cannons to four 30-mm Aden cannons in a detachable gun pack located in the lower fuselage behind the pilot's cockpit. The gun pack could be replaced in a few minutes by a fully loaded pack under the forward fuselage. The P1067 was better armed than the competing North American F-86 Sabre, which had six nose-mounted 0.5-inch machine guns with a much lower destructive capability.

By April 1949, following the construction of a mock-up in the Kingston experimental department, the basic overall design was established, initiating the creation of some 40,000 jigs and fixtures, using external subcontractors. Achieving a priority was a problem, and initial production was only achieved by using interim tools for detail parts, constructed by skilled fitters rather than toolmakers, who were in short supply. Major assembly jigs needed to be made to a higher standard, and eventually they were acquired from Macchi, Breda and Fiat in Italy.

Calling on their Second World War experience in volume production, Hawker divided the airframe into major individual fully equipped assemblies. This approach was also designed to make the provision of spares more convenient. These assemblies were to be of convenient size for transportation and each consist of a series of sub-assemblies. The major breakdown of the airframe was in six parts. These were the front, centre and rear fuselage, tail section and the two wings. The front fuselage section consisted of the cockpit, nose wheel, armament pack, radar-ranging system and camera gun. The centre fuselage included the integral wing roots, air intake ducts and engine supports. The detachable rear fuselage housed the removable jet pipe, the fin mounting base and tail cone. The tail unit was a single assembly and the main planes were complete with undercarriage legs. All these units had to be fully interchangeable as they were sourced from throughout the entire Hawker Siddeley Group and, additionally, from suppliers of specialist systems and equipment. With no airfield in Kingston, the major assemblies were shipped for final assembly at the newly acquired ex-RAF airfield at Dunsfold in Surrey, some 30 miles from Kingston. Wartime Hawker fighter production had been at a major factory at Langley, but the airfield was restricted both in ground space for jet operations and air space with the growth of Heathrow Airport.

Work started on the construction of the first prototype in late 1949, with the other two prototypes following in the next year. Eight months before the first aircraft was due to fly, instructions were placed with Hawker Aircraft at Kingston to plan for the production of 200 Avon-powered aircraft. Soon afterwards, similar instructions were received by Armstrong Whitworth Aircraft at Coventry for 200 Sapphire-powered examples. The first aircraft, WB188, was unarmed and featured an anti-spin parachute in a tail fairing. This aircraft concentrated on aerodynamic development, while the second prototype, WB195, was fully representative of the early production standard. It had both the Aden guns and a ranging radar fitted. Both these prototypes were Avon powered, but the third prototype, WB202, was fitted with a Sapphire engine.

By April 1950, the first prototype airframe had been completed. While Dunsfold was being prepared as an assembly and test facility, the prototype P1067 WB188 was dismantled at Kingston and taken by road to the Aeroplane & Armament Experimental Establishment (A&AEE) at Boscombe Down in June 1951. The aircraft was painted in an attractive duck-egg green and the first Avon engine run was on 1 July, followed by taxi trials during which a brake fault resulted in the aircraft veering off the runway during a fast taxi run.

With the sad death of Wimpy Wade in the P1081, his deputy, Neville Duke, was promoted to chief test pilot. Duke already had considerable experience with Hawker's earlier jet aircraft. Following some high-speed runs along the Boscombe runway, the aircraft was refuelled and took off in the afternoon on 20 July for its first forty-seven-minute flight. Duke was entirely happy with the aircraft, which by this time had been named Hunter. On the first test flight Duke took the aircraft up to 32,000 feet for some gentle handling tests. He then descended to 10,000 feet where he conducted stall testing at various flap settings, with the undercarriage retracted and lowered to check handling in the landing configuration. Speed was limited to Mach 0.88, and Duke stated that the aircraft handled extremely well. There was some concern with high fuel consumption, but this was explained by a modest leak in the rear fuselage tank. One of the new features of the Hunter was the use of power controls, which worked well once adjusted.

According to Neville Duke, the Hunter flew smoothly from the start. Flight testing was approached with great caution, starting with taxi tests along the runway to check brakes and ground handling, gradually working up to take-off speed. When ground handling had been approved, the aircraft was lifted off the runway for short ground hops to assess basic controls handling and to establish

Hunter prototype under construction in the experimental shop at Kingston. (*RAF Museum*)

Hunter prototype WB188 flown for the first time by Neville Duke on 20 July 1951. (*BAE Systems*)

the correct trim for take-off. When everything was satisfactory, the first flight was made, and Duke felt at home in the aircraft immediately. The early flights were made to identify any faults with general handling, to conduct level speed tests and to measure the rate of climb, stability, manoeuvrability, and other parameters. Following each test flight Duke reported the results to the design and maintenance teams, and modifications were embodied and tested. These preliminary flight tests took many flying hours over the course of six months; only then could the Hunter be taken supersonic and up to 40,000 feet altitude.

Following further test flights, the aircraft was transferred to Farnborough on 10 August, which was closer to Kingston. At Farnborough, test flying continued for four weeks while work was completed on preparations at Dunsfold, where the testing moved on 7 September 1951. Within a month of the first flight, speeds in excess of 700 mph were being achieved, and in September, with only eleven flying hours completed, the aircraft was demonstrated at the annual Farnborough Air Show.

Neville Duke had experienced very active combat service during the Second World War. He started his RAF flying training at White Waltham as a LAC pilot u/t and was soon promoted to acting corporal, flying in Tiger Moths. He made his first flight on 20 August 1940 and went solo on 6 September after eight and a half hours' tuition, just as the Battle of Britain was reaching its climax. His next step in flying training was to join 5 Flying Training School (FTS) at Sealand, flying the more advanced Miles Master with additional controls, including a retractable undercarriage. The syllabus there included navigation, cross-country flying on instruments, and aerobatics. With a move to Tern Hill, Duke was selected as a potential officer and moved into the officers' mess. In February 1941 he gained his wings and was commissioned as pilot officer. Duke wanted to be selected as a fighter pilot, so when a posting to 58 OTU at Grangemouth came through with the chance of flying Spitfires alongside instructors who were Battle of Britain veterans, he was delighted. He flew a Spitfire I on 2 March and overshot on landing, tipping the aircraft up on its nose, but he was allowed to complete the six-week course. Training included practice formation flying, dogfighting, aerobatics, instrument flying, mock attacks and firing machine guns. With an overall total of 145 hours and fifty minutes, of which twenty-six hours and ten minutes were in a Spitfire, Duke was ready to join an operational squadron.

Duke's first choice was to join a squadron at Biggin Hill on the front line. In 1941 the airfield was in very poor condition with no hangar intact, but for Duke it brought back memories of when, as a boy, he had visited the airfield on one of the pre-war Empire Air Days. The wing, based at Biggin Hill, was led by Wing Commander 'Sailor' Malan DSO, DFC, a South African who had fought in the Battle of Britain. The RAF was moving from the defensive to offensive and Duke joined 92 Squadron, which was the top-scoring squadron in 11 Group with 135 enemy aircraft destroyed. Duke made his first claim on 23 June with a Bf 109 damaged, and the following day he claimed a Bf 109 as a victory.

In November 1941 Duke was posted to the Middle East for a nominal six weeks, which turned out to be three years. He departed from Plymouth in a

Above: Neville Duke, Hawker chief test pilot, after making the first flight of the Hunter prototype from Boscombe Down. (*RAF Museum*)

Right: Hunter prototype WB188 head-on, showing its classic clean lines. (*BAE Systems*)

Sunderland, and many of the sixteen men who accompanied him on board were
never to see England again. The first stop was Gibraltar after passing the well-lit
coastline of Portugal, and then on to Malta and Cairo in a Wellington. Duke
joined 112 Squadron flying P-40s alongside 250 RAF Squadron and 3 RAAF
Squadron, which completed the wing, tasked with the air defence of the allied
army in North Africa. Duke was unfamiliar with the P-40 and pranged one on his
first flight. Its performance was inferior to that of the Spitfire, but in December
the P-40s were replaced by the improved Tomahawks. In March 1942, Duke was
awarded an immediate DFC and soon afterwards his operational tour ended. He
had competed 161 sorties, flying 120 hours. In April he was posted to the fighter
school at El Ballah by the Suez Canal as an instructor.

On 18 November 1942, Duke rejoined his old 92 Squadron, which had recently
arrived in the Middle East equipped with Tomahawks. Many of the ground crew
from Biggin Hill and Gravesend were still with the squadron. In a few months,
while Rommel's Afrika Korps was in retreat from the Eighth Army and Desert Air
Force, Duke was again becoming tour expired; he made his last operation on 11
May 1943 as escort for American Kittyhawks on a bombing raid. During his second
tour he had destroyed fourteen enemy aircraft, making a total of twenty-two, with
many others either destroyed or damaged. His operational flying hours for his
second tour amounted to 202, making a total of 424 hours in two tours, flying 293
sorties. He had hoped to be returning back to Britain, but instead he was promoted
to squadron leader as chief flying instructor at 73 OTU at Abu Suweir. Despite the
initial disappointment of not going home, Duke enjoyed training new pilots in the
skills of combat and was relieved, at least, to have secured a flying posting.

Duke's posting back to the Desert Air Force came through at the end of February
1944. He took over 145 Squadron as commanding officer, and was to be flying
in the same wing as 92 Squadron, which by now was equipped with Spitfires. His
second day with 145 Squadron was almost his last when a shell splinter punched
a hole in his starboard wing, damaging the leading edge. He was afterwards
awarded a second bar to his DFC. On 7 June 1944, Duke's Spitfire was hit in
the radiator by ground fire and he had to abandon the aircraft. He parachuted
into Lake Bracciano, where he was rescued by two Italian boys. Again Duke was
becoming tour expired. His final operation was on 20 September, completing a
third tour of 288 hours on 486 sorties. His final score was twenty-eight enemy
aircraft destroyed, with three probables and five damaged. On 27 October he was
posted to Britain, just three days short of three years since his departure from
Plymouth. Finally, he returned to his home in Tonbridge.

On return to Britain, Duke had no desire for an RAF desk job and began looking
into ways in which he could continue to fly. He was fortunate to be offered the
chance to take on production test flying and was introduced to Philip Lucas, the
chief test pilot of Hawker Aircraft at Langley. He was offered the job testing
production Tempest IIs and Vs and started on New Year's Day in 1945. In August
1945 he was offered a permanent commission in the RAF and had no hesitation
in accepting it as it would allow him to take the ETPS (Empire Test Pilots' School)

course. He was accepted after spending a year at Hawker Aircraft. Soon after his twenty-fourth birthday, Duke joined the No. 4 Course of the ETPS at Cranfield, which enabled him to move on from production testing to experimental flying. Halfway through the course, Duke was offered the opportunity to join the High Speed Flight at Tangmere where Group Captain Teddy Donaldson had achieved 616 mph in a Meteor, increasing the world record by 10 mph, which was close to the Meteor's limit. Following completion of the ETPS course, Duke was posted to the A&AEE at Boscombe Down, testing new types before they entered operational service. In June 1948, having been offered a position as experimental test pilot at Hawker, Duke resigned his RAF commission. In August he joined Hawker.

Wimpy Wade was the chief test pilot at Hawker, but after his death and the mysterious loss of the P1081 prototype VX279 on 3 April 1951, Duke was appointed chief test pilot with responsibility for flight testing the new Hunter. Duke and his wife Gwen moved into a cottage close to the perimeter track at the newly acquired Second World War airfield at Dunsfold.

When the prototype Hunter arrived at Dunsfold, the original Avon engine was replaced by a production-standard 6,500-lb-thrust RA.7. When flying continued, performance testing was gradually expanded, including climbs to 40,000 feet. Rather unexpectedly, when approaching M 0.97, supersonic speed, there was airframe buffet and severe rudder vibration. Duke took WB188 to M 1.3 indicated in a dive, but the reading was unreliable due to the effects of shockwaves around the pitot head. There was concern that the Hunter was unable to achieve its predicted safe limiting speed. Various modifications were tried to exceed M 0.97, and success was achieved on 6 June 1952 when a bullet fairing was installed in the trailing edge of the fin/tailplane junction. This gave the first vibration-free high-speed flight passing Mach 1, although the sound barrier had been officially broken in April. With the new fairing fitted, the Hunter was able to reach Mach 1.06 in a 30-degree dive from 45,000 feet, although it was not until 24 June in a dive from 30,000 feet to 15,000 feet that the Hawker team experienced a very audible sonic boom.

The Korean War started on 25 June 1950, and Britain was part of the United Nations forces called in to help resolve the conflict. The British contribution was relatively small, with the main effort being carrier-based fighter bombers, which required protection by American fighters. The RAF did not have any aircraft capable of intercepting the communist-operated MiG-15 swept-wing jet fighters, and following RAAF experience with Meteors in the conflict, it was obvious that the first-generation Gloster design was ineffective. Since the end of the Second World War, Britain had experienced an economic depression, but when Churchill's government was re-elected in October 1951, spending priority was given to Britain's defences with the initiation of the 'super priority' production programme. This programme pushed promising aircraft projects rapidly into production, with essential modifications catching up when possible. The Hawker Hunter became part of this programme. It aimed to return combat aircraft production to wartime levels, but the industry had become so reduced in capacity that, in reality, it was simply not possible to expand the capability.

Neville Duke brings the prototype Hunter WB188 close in to the camera aircraft. (*BAE Systems*)

WB195, the second 7,550-lb-thrust Avon-powered prototype, fitted with a gun pack and radar-ranging system, was flown for the first time from Dunsfold by Neville Duke on 5 May 1952. It was the beginning of a prolonged handling and performance evaluation, with additional trials flown from ministry and RAF establishments. During the early flight trials the Ministry of Supply requested the incorporation of an air brake for operation at all speeds and altitudes without affecting the gun-aiming characteristics of the aircraft. The second prototype was allocated to this programme as the low drag and sleek lines of the Hunter were good for high performance, but deceleration was required to bring the aircraft within combat limitations. When the first production Hunters were flying, the air brake configuration had still to be decided. A number of configurations were tested, but most resulted in a sharp nose-down pitch when deployed. An acceptable answer was to fit a forward-hinged brake under the fuselage just aft of the wing trailing edge.

The third prototype, WB202, was first flown by Duke on 30 November 1952 from Dunsfold, powered by an 8,000-lb-thrust Sa.6 Sapphire turbojet, making it in effect the prototype F.2. Following the formal flight development, WB202 was experimentally fitted with four dummy Firestreak guided missiles under the wings for handling trials at Dunsfold. The first batch of production Hunters had already been 'ordered off the drawing board' with the issue of an instruction to proceed (ITP) on 20 October 1950 covering 198 aircraft at a total unit cost of £172,000. With the possible benefits of the government-declared 'super priority' production system, the manufacturing rate was increased, which allowed the first production F.1 WT555 to be flown from Dunsfold on 16 May 1953, a year after the second prototype.

Assembly of the second Hunter prototype, WB195, at Kingston. (*RAF Museum*)

The second prototype Hunter, WB195, was first flown by Neville Duke on 5 May 1952. (*BAE Systems*)

The second Hunter prototype, WB195, was more representative of the production standard with armament fitted. (*BAE Systems*)

The third Hunter prototype, WB202, being assembled at Kingston. (*RAF Museum*)

The third Hunter prototype, WB202, at Dunsfold. It was powered by an Armstrong Siddeley Sapphire turbojet. (*RAF Museum*)

The first production Hunter F.1, WT555, was first flown on 16 May 1953. (*BAE Systems*)

Being such a totally new concept in fighter design, a large number of the early production Hunters were allocated to a range of development programmes leading to service entry with the RAF. With only three prototypes, one of which was just an aerodynamic aircraft, the broad range of trials required a significant number of potentially combat-ready early aircraft, which should have been ordered with the prototypes, causing delays in eventual service entry. Lessons learned with the Hunter resulted in later aircraft being ordered with at least twenty aircraft in a pre-production batch, in addition to the prototypes, to achieve the full range of service trials and development. Many of these aircraft only entered service for the initial training of air and ground crews, while others were used for further systems development. Meanwhile, to hasten production, Hawker took over a Second World War shadow factory at Blackpool Squires Gate, where there was an adequate runway. At the same time, at Baginton, Coventry, Armstrong Whitworth set up for the initial F.2 production batch of forty-five aircraft.

Production facilities at Coventry were far superior to the Hawker factories around Kingston. At Armstrong Whitworth, manufacture, assembly and flight testing were all achieved at Baginton, while the Sapphire engines were produced by the associate Armstrong Siddeley. At Hawker, sub-assemblies were manufactured at Kingston and delivered for assembly to the Second World War factory at Langley, before being taken apart again for transport and reassembly at Dunsfold, ready for flight testing.

Initially, the overall Hunter flight development progressed with no major problems, and this allowed the Hawker design team to look at improvements in performance and endurance. A study was initiated under project P1083 to achieve supersonic in level flight for the basic Hunter, with a 50-degree swept-back wing and increased power from a reheat Rolls-Royce Avon RA.14 turbojet. Manufacture of the new wings was started at Kingston in October 1952, and with more representative aircraft available for flight testing, WB188 was withdrawn from test flying to be fitted with a reheat Avon and additional wing-located fuel tanks. The final configuration of an air brake had still not been decided, and the wing-mounted versions had been abandoned. The original prototype was therefore fitted with twin clam-shell air brakes on either side of the rear fuselage.

In July 1953, with the end of the Korean War approaching, the Air Ministry withdrew the 'super priority' programme and began to revert back to the previous short-term economic plan. As a result, work on the supersonic Hunter development was no longer required, and work on the construction of what would have been the prototype WN470 was stopped on 13 July 1953. This left Hawker with a much-modified prototype, WB188, and no effective requirement.

Despite this setback, the Hawker design team decided to use the aircraft as a private venture in the study of future reheat jet engine developments. By further improving WB188, they sought to break the world absolute air speed record. The benefit of the resultant publicity was also a consideration. The speed record at the time was held by a North American F-86D Sabre at 715.15 mph. Rolls-Royce undertook to provide a racing version of the RA.7R Avon, with a dry thrust of

Hunter sub-assembly manufacture at Kingston. (*RAF Museum*)

Hunter Mk 1 manufacture at Langley. (*RAF Museum*)

Hunter Mk 1 assembly at Langley before moving by road to Dunsfold for final assembly and flight testing. (*RAF Museum*)

6,750 lb, increasing to 9,500 lb with reheat. Aerodynamic improvements included a sharply pointed nose cone, a smoother curved windscreen and the removal of the new air brakes to keep drag to a minimum. With these modifications, WB188 became the sole Hunter Mk 3. It was resprayed in an overall red colour scheme.

With preparations completed, WB188 was flown to Tangmere for the first practice flight on 31 August 1953. Tangmere was selected as a base because it was adjacent to the route off the south coast from the pier at Bognor past Littlehampton and Worthing, where Duke had been a member of the RAF High Speed Flight in 1946, the year Teddy Donaldson established a record of 616 mph in a Gloster Meteor. On this first practice flight, Duke reached 722.5 mph in less than ideal weather conditions, but on the second day the flight had to be abandoned due to the starboard main undercarriage leg dropping at between 550 and 600 mph while flying at low level. Despite the stress on the airframe, the aircraft remained controllable and was flying again after only six days on the ground. On its next flight, Duke flew WB188 to a new speed record of 727.6 mph, averaged over three runs along the course. Soon after, on 19 September, Duke took WB188 round a 100-km closed circuit course to set a new world record for this course at 709.2 mph.

Following these successes, the prototype was withdrawn from flying use. Fortunately, a task was found for it as a technical training aircraft at RAF Halton

Hunter prototype WB188 modified for the absolute speed record in overall red finish and with a curved windscreen. This aircraft, the sole F.3, also featured air brakes on both sides of the rear fuselage, but they were not adopted. (*BAE Systems*)

Neville Duke in the cockpit of the record-breaking Hunter WB188 at Dunsfold. (*BAE Systems*)

Neville Duke by Hunter F.3 WB188 following his speed record success from Tangmere. (*RAF Museum*)

in November 1954, and on completion of those duties it was set up as gate guard at RAF Melksham. It was then saved by the RAF Colerne Aviation Museum, and when that closed it went to St Athan and the RAF Museum at Cosford. Since September 1992 it has been on loan to the Tanmere Military Aviation Museum, displayed in its record-breaking markings.

With production only slowly building up and the first production Hunter joining flight development in May 1953, the withdrawal of WB188 left the bulk of the flight testing on the remaining two prototypes. The Sapphire-powered F.2 prototype, WB202, was finished in RAF-standard overall silver finish and was allocated to gun-firing trials. Gun ground firings were done into the gun butts in February 1953 and air firings were achieved at Boscombe Down the next month. Despite concerns that spent cartridge cases from the Aden guns might cause damage to the aircraft, the gun-firing trials went very well, and the aircraft was returned for air brake installation, which was still unresolved. The clam shell air brakes installed on WB188 had caused an unacceptable nose-down pitch when operated. The position chosen under the fuselage, meanwhile, did not allow enough room for the brake to be flush when retracted. In addition to WB202, the twelfth production Hunter, F.1 WT566, was also allocated to the air brake trials. After much adjustment an air brake was mounted on the outer skin with a maximum deflection of 67 degrees. The final configuration was established in June 1954. Because of the under fuselage position, the air brake could not be deployed on approach to land and was locked up when the undercarriage was lowered.

With the first production Hunter joining the flight development programme, the next twenty or so aircraft were allocated to the various programmes with Hawker, Rolls-Royce and government establishments in 1953 and 1954. These included armament trials, expansion of the flight envelope and systems development. Aerodynamic development included extended wing leading edges on WT568, fuel drop tank trials on WT569 and blown flaps on WT656. WT571 had bulged fairings over the rear fuselage to investigate the 'Area Rule', but the increase in performance was disappointing. Aircraft were allocated to specialist establishments to develop operational criteria, including the compilation of 'pilot's notes'. Training schemes for pilots and ground crews also had to be established. Early Hunters were stored for the short term at 5 MU Kemble while service testing progressed, but on 1 July 1953 an interim certificate of release was issued to allow deliveries from Kemble to the Central Fighter Establishment (CFE) at West Raynham. This allowed evaluation flights to start by the unit's experienced pilots. One of the first activities was participation in Exercise Dividend, in which Hunters were able to intercept USAF B-45s and B-47s, as well as the previously unattainable RAF Canberra jet bombers.

During this exercise one of the more serious deficiencies was discovered in the Hunter. Due to insufficient fuel capacity, the aircraft was limited to operations within just 80 miles of West Raynham. The existing fuel capacity of 80 gallons was obviously totally inadequate. No provision for additional internal fuel capacity had been investigated by Hawker, although the company were aware that endurance

The second production Hunter F.1, WT556, was used in the flight development programme to complement the three prototypes. (*RAF Museum*)

Hunter F.1 WT557 was also used for flight development. (*RAF Museum*)

Hunter F.1 WT571 was modified with a 'coke-bottle' rear fuselage shape to test the area rule, but this was not adopted. (*BAE Systems*)

Rear view of Hunter F.1 WT571, modified with area-rule fuselage. (*RAF Museum*)

Hunter F.1 WT594 was an early production example used for systems development and service trials, as well as air brake development. It was delivered to 5 MU on 17 September 1954 and later served with 222 and 43 Squadrons. (*RAF Museum*)

Frank Bullen was a member of the test pilot team at Dunsfold. (*RAF Museum*)

was not to specification. While external drop tanks were a possibility, only WB202 had been fitted with dummy underwing tanks for aerodynamic purposes. The original specification that called for no more than 20 per cent of remaining fuel to be lost if the tanks were penetrated by one bullet was not achieved either. The CFE pilots reported misting and icing of the canopy at high altitudes, which dangerously reduced visibility. However, the most important problem occurred when the Aden cannons were fired: the Avon engine was incompatible, while the Sapphire engine presented no problems when the cannons were fired.

When firing the guns the evaluation pilots were surprised that the Avons suffered violent engine surging due to the ingestion of the Aden's exhaust gases. It occurred without any obvious warning in a variety of potential combat situations when the aircraft was above 25,000 feet and at speeds in excess of 400 mph. With a serious problem on their hands, Hawker devised a short-term solution: to automatically reduce fuel flow to the engine whenever the guns were fired, which was hardly ideal in combat. Firing the cannons also produced a significant nose-down pitch, making the aircraft a less than ideal weapons platform, although it was helpful that the Sapphire engine was not affected in the same way: the gun-firing trials with the F.2 went very well. Unfortunately the gun-firing problems with the Hunter F.1 were not fully resolved until later marks were developed with more robust Avon engines.

Neville Duke continued to lead the Hunter flight development team, facing the hazards of test flying. In August 1955 he was carrying out gun-firing tests at low level off Littlehampton at 700 mph. All of a sudden there was a loud bang which shook the aircraft; he reduced power immediately to check the instruments. There were no obvious problems, but as he began to increase power again, the engine was very rough when the temperature rose rapidly. Following this, the engine stopped altogether. Duke began to glide back towards Ford in an effort to save the aircraft. He achieved this, and the problem was identified as turbine blade failure due to engine surge when the 30-mm cannons were fired. For saving the aircraft Duke was awarded the Queen's Commendation for Valuable Service in the Air.

Two days later, when the engine had been replaced, Duke returned to Ford to collect the Hunter. Take-off was normal up to 1,000 feet with Chichester harbour below, but opening the throttle only gave idling thrust. With RAF Thorney Island almost directly below, Duke reduced height. However, due to his position, he arrived with too much airspeed for a normal landing but not enough for a normal circuit. Losing height, he put the aircraft down across the airfield on the rough grass surface where it bounced violently. To reduce the run, Duke selected the undercarriage up, but only one main wheel retracted. Sitting helplessly in the cockpit, Duke jettisoned the canopy and cut the fuel: the aircraft careered in a number of arcs until it reached the airfield boundary across a ditch and hit the sea wall. The aircraft disintegrated, but Duke climbed out of the wreck. He had cuts and bruises and was aching badly: he was later found to have fractured his spine. The fault which caused the engine problem was a small particle of fluff in a fuel control valve.

Duke was on his back in a plaster cast for some months. He eventually returned to test flying while still wearing plaster, and although he still suffered discomfort in his back he appeared to be recovering well and continued to clear the gun-firing problems. Then, on 9 May 1956, a heavy landing in the P1099 crushed a disc in his back and even dislodged some teeth fillings. Duke was back on his back again, in extreme pain. He was flying again in October 1956, but was unable to tolerate more than limited 'g' forces, and he sadly resigned after many happy years with Hawker.

A further problem with the Hunter was damage from the ejected gun cartridges. Trials with cannons fitted in the nose of a Beaufighter had suggested the possibility of the same problem with the Hunter, but it was hoped that the heavier 30-mm Aden cannon cartridges would fall away clear of the airframe. However, during service testing of the guns it was found that the ejected lighter links were hitting the fuselage's underside and causing damage. To overcome the problem, the Hunter had distinctive fairings fitted under the guns known as 'Sabrinas', in recognition of a well-endowed television actress of the time. These fairings collected the links and the heavier cartridge cases were allowed to fall clear.

A considerable amount of testing was done with the Aden gun pack, which when fired caused a punishing reaction in the airframe's structure. When all four guns were fired together, structural cracks rapidly formed in the forward fuselage, and therefore aircraft were restricted to firing only two guns at a time, until stainless steel reinforcements could be incorporated on the production line. Once established in service, the Aden gun pack was a very effective weapon, and well in advance of any guns in use previously.

With Hunter F.1 production well advanced, it was clear that the aircraft was a great improvement over earlier types, although it still suffered from a number of unresolved development problems. With hindsight, these would have been solved by a pre-production batch. The CFE continued service trials with due consideration to the known deficiencies, but even their pilots were caught out by the seriously short endurance. A major incident occurred on 8 February 1956 when six students and two instructors from the Day Fighter Leader School (DFLS) departed from West Raynham for an air combat exercise at 45,000 feet. Weather conditions were not good, but the forecast suggested an improvement, although the Air Fighting Development School (AFDS) had cancelled flying for the day.

After a relatively brief but successful mock dogfight, the Hunters began their return to base. At 20,000 feet over West Raynham, the weather worsened with a 400-foot cloud base and fog that restricted visibility to only 1,000 yards. With only twenty minutes of fuel remaining, the pilots elected to divert to Marham, descending in pairs to 2,000 feet, thirty seconds apart. Unfortunately the weather at Marham had also begun to deteriorate rapidly with the fog over the ground under the low cloud base. The first pair emerged from the cloud base to be faced with the fog bank. The leader made an overshoot, but the number 2 made a successful landing after being in the air for forty-two minutes. The leader made three circuits before locating the airfield and landing safely, running out of fuel as he turned off the runway. Of the next pair, the first pilot only caught occasional sight of the ground and climbed away to eject, while his number 2 continued his approach, but crashed in a field a couple of miles short of the Marham runway. The next pair leader made one low approach without success, and with very low fuel, climbed away and ejected. The pilot following made a low approach, but climbed away when trees obstructed his path, and made a circuit at 150 feet when his engine stopped and he landed straight ahead with no power. The two remaining Hunters were abandoned by their pilots when they ran out of fuel. Six Hunters were destroyed and one pilot killed due to a basic lack of sufficient endurance, which should have lasted for at least one hour.

3

Entry into RAF Service

The Hunter was introduced to RAF operational service by 43 Squadron, the 'Fighting Cocks', based at Leuchars. The first four F.1s were delivered to this squadron in July 1954, replacing Meteor F.8s. With additional deliveries arriving up to October, the squadron was able to start operational flying, and despite the aircraft's well-known faults, which included gun-related engine flame-outs, the service experiences recorded by pilots were positive. As a sign of confidence in the aircraft, a four-aircraft display team was created, with operations restricted to the established limits, to gain experience while awaiting the arrival of the more effective Hunter marks.

By the end of 1954, 139 Hunter F.1s had been completed at Kingston with a further twenty-six from Blackpool, allowing two more squadrons to form within Fighter Command. In December 1954, 222 Squadron, based at Leuchars, began to receive Hunter F.1s to replace their Meteors, while Odiham-based 54 Squadron received their first Hunters in February 1955. These were replaced by F.4s in September. In consideration of the F.1's range restriction, it was decided not to re-equip Germany-based RAF squadrons until a more suitable version was available. Meanwhile, UK-based Hunter F.1 flying was kept within easy flying range of the manufacturing sites and maintenance units in case of emergency. A comprehensive training organisation was created with 229 Operational Conversion Unit (OCU) at Chivenor, which became the major Hunter pilot training organisation from April 1955 until September 1974, when the tactical weapons unit (TWU) at Brawdy took over this role. In addition, 233 OCU was formed at Pembrey in December 1952 to train fighter pilots, initially on Vampires and later on Hunter F.1s, until it was disbanded in September 1957. Hunter F.1s were also delivered to the Empire Test Pilots' School (ETPS) at Farnborough, and Fighter Weapons School (FWS) at Leconfield.

The introduction of Sapphire-powered Hunter F.2s was much easier due to there being no Aden gun firing problems, although lack of endurance was still a problem. With more thrust from the engine, the F.2 had slightly improved performance with 698 mph at sea level compared with the 693 mph of the F.1.

Hunter F.1 WT588 first flew on 24 February 1954. It served with the CFE and AFDS before delivery to 43 Squadron at Leuchars, coded P, later in the same year. (*RAF Museum*)

Hunter F.1 WT613 first flew on 16 July 1954 and was delivered to 5 MU on 5 August 1954. From there it was issued to 43 Squadron at Leuchars. It also served with DFLS. (*Newark Air Museum*)

A formation of Hunter F.1s in 43 Squadron. (*RAF Museum*)

Hunter F.4 WV387 of 43 Squadron in April 1957, with revised squadron markings. (*RAF Museum*)

No. 54 Squadron Hunter F.1 WW636 leads a formation of two RCAF F-86 Sabres with the Sky Lancer team and a USAF T-33 of the Aerojets team. (*RAF*)

Hunter F.1 WT638 first flew on 7 September 1954 and was initially delivered to 222 Squadron on 3 January 1955. It was issued to 233 OCU at Pembrey on 13 January 1956 with the code G. (*Newark Air Museum*)

Hunter F.1 WT577 first flew on 19 January 1954 and was delivered to the CFE on 5 July 1954, and was used by the AFDS. It was written off on 20 August 1956. (*Newark Air Museum*)

Hunter F.1 WT628 first flew on 5 August 1954 and was delivered to 5 MU on 27 September. It was issued to ETPS at Farnborough and crashed due to fuel starvation at Cove near Farnborough on 18 July 1955, killing the pilot. (*Newark Air Museum*)

A pair of Hunter F.4s, XF940 and XF969, with the ETPS. (*RAF Museum*)

The F.2 also had a better rate of climb. It became clear that the Sapphire should have been the primary engine for the Hunter as it was less expensive and more reliable than the Avon. Only forty-five F.2s were assembled at Coventry. Deliveries started in September 1954 to 257 Squadron at Wattisham, with a move to Wymeswold on 10 June 1956 and back to Wattisham on 15 January 1957, where the squadron was disbanded on 31 March of that year. In February 1955 the first F.2s were delivered to 263 Squadron, also at Wattisham, but were exchanged for the improved F.5s in May. Other service testing establishments, including the CFE, also received F.2s.

The Hunter F.1s and F.2s were an interim standard to give Fighter Command pilots and ground crews experience in working with a modern transonic combat fighter. Within their limitations, the F.1s and F.2s were flown intensively. In January 1956, 43 Squadron was allocated to additional firing development with the Aden cannons. This came with an initial restrictive height band of between 20,000 and 25,000 feet, which was later relaxed down to sea level, and speeds of up to around 633 mph, the equivalent of 550 knots. The trials were so intensive that the ground crews at Leuchars struggled to maintain serviceability, which finally resulted in the trials being terminated. In addition to 43 Squadron, 54 Squadron also formed an aerobatic team.

Once the student pilots at Chivenor had completed their basic and advanced flying training, the role of the 229 OCU was to teach the operation of the Hunter as a weapons platform following conversion to type. At this stage there was no Hunter dual trainer, and students had jet experience only in Vampire T.11s and some single-seat Vampire FB.5s. The Hunter presented a major advance in jet-fighter performance, but its low endurance remained a major concern. No. 233 OCU at Pembrey was formed to share the high initial workload caused by the high demand for Hunter pilots.

With only five RAF squadrons equipped with interim Hunter F.1s and F.2s, there was an urgent need to increase the fuel capacity. It was decided, therefore, not only to increase internal fuel capacity from 337 to 414 gallons, but also to incorporate wing strong points and plumbing for pylon-mounted 100-gallon drop tanks. Later fuel drop tanks could also be carried on outer wing pylons, increasing the overall fuel capacity to 814 gallons. This gave a practical ferry range as the Hunter was not equipped for air-to-air refuelling. Weapons were also to be incorporated for use on ground-attack sorties. The resulting improved F.4 WT701 was the 114th aircraft off the Kingston production line. The twenty-seventh from Blackpool was also built to the new standard. A total of 365 Hunter F.4s were produced from both Hawker factories, with the first flying on 20 October 1954. With the tension rising in East–West relations and the threat of the Cold War looming, the US government introduced the Offshore Procurement Bill which allocated funds to European defence programmes. The Hunter F.4 was a beneficiary and was paid for by America. The first 156 Hunter F.4s retained the Avon 113, but subsequent aircraft were powered by the Avon 115, which was modified to avoid surging during gun firing. Most of the earlier aircraft, which had been put into storage, were modified retrospectively.

A formation of 257 Squadron Hunter F.2s: WN950 F, WN915 I, WN948 R and WN952 G.
(*RAF Museum*)

Hunter F.2s WN915 and WN948 with 257 Squadron based at Wattisham, May 1955. (*RAF Museum*)

A formation of Hunter F.2s of 257 Squadron based at Wattisham, with WN950 nearest. (*RAF Museum*)

Right: Hunter F.2s of 263 Squadron lined up at Wattisham, headed by WN900 which also operated with 257 Squadron from 16 January 1957. It was withdrawn to 5 MU Kemble on 15 April 1957. (*RAF Museum*)

Below: Hunter F.2s and F.5s with 263 Squadron at Wattisham in 1955, including WN946 N, WN947 R, WN983 and WN980. (*RAF Museum*)

Hunter F.5s with 263 Squadron at Wahn in 1956 being prepared for flight. (*RAF Museum*)

Hunter F.1s of 54 Squadron, which formed its own formation aerobatic team. (*Author's collection*)

Hunter F.1 WT614 B of 229 OCU at Leconfield, September 1956. (*Vic Flintham collection*)

A Hunter F.4 of 145 Squadron, 229 OCU. (*Newark Air Museum*)

The first unit to receive replacement F.4s for F.1s was 247 Squadron, based at Odiham, in May 1955. No. 54 Squadron, also based at Odiham, followed in September of that year. No. 111 Squadron at North Weald took first deliveries of F.4s in June 1955, replacing its Meteor F.8s. Further to this, the following Fighter Command squadrons took deliveries of the F.4: 43 Squadron at Leuchars in February 1956; 66 and 92 Squadrons at Linton-on-Ouse in March and April 1956 respectively; 222 Squadron at Leuchars in August 1956 (replacing its F.1s—this unit was disbanded on 1 November 1957); 74 and 72 Squadrons at Horsham St Faith in March and April 1957 respectively; and finally (for UK-based squadrons) 245 Squadron at Stradishall in April 1957.

Meanwhile Hunters were being delivered to the 2nd Tactical Air Force (TAF) in Germany. No. 98 Squadron at Jever was the first foreign-based unit to receive them in April 1955 (this squadron was disbanded on 25 July 1957), and a month later, 118 Squadron, also based at Jever, received a delivery of F.4s. No. 14 Squadron at Oldenburg re-equipped in June 1955, as did 26 Squadron, replacing its Sabres. In July 1955 IV Squadron, based at Jever, re-equipped with F.4s and 20 Squadron, at Oldenburg, received theirs in November. In January 1956, 67 Squadron at Brüggen and 93 Squadron at Jever received deliveries of Hunter F.4s, the latter unit replacing its Sabres. At Brüggen, 71, 112 and 130 Squadrons replaced all their Sabres with F.4s in April 1956, and the following month, when 3 and 234 Squadrons took delivery of Hunter F.4s at Geilenkirchen, the programme to replace the American-supplied interim Sabre was completed. Eventually nine UK-based squadrons and thirteen 2nd TAF squadrons were operating Hunter F.4s, although some for a only

Hunter F.4 WT795 of 247 Squadron first flew on 21 April 1955 and was delivered to 247 Squadron on 4 May 1955. It was moved to 229 OCU and finally broken up by HAL in September 1964. (*RAF Museum*)

Hunter F.4 WT775 Q of 247 Squadron. (*Vic Flintham collection*)

Hunter F.4s with 54 Squadron based at Odiham in 1956, led by the CO's aircraft XE659 'OWF'. (*RAF Museum*)

Hunter F.4s, including WT716, of 111 Squadron, practicing aerobatics in 1956. (*Vic Flintham collection*)

Hunter F.4 WV409 with 66 Squadron during transition from Sabres. It is photographed here in a mixed formation with Sabre XD753 and Meteor F.8 WK158. (*RAF Museum*)

Hunter F.4 XF324 D of 92 Squadron at RAF Burtonwood, May 1956. (*Air Britain*)

Hunter F.4 XE679 was delivered to 5 MU on 4 July 1955 and was issued to 111 Squadron. It transferred to 222 Squadron on 4 December 1956 until retiring to Kemble on 5 November 1957. It was moved to Halton 1 SofTT as 7887M, where it retained the 222 Squadron markings. It was returned to HAL in September 1971 for conversion to Mk 74B for Singapore, where it was delivered on 13 June 1973. (*Philip Birtles*)

Hunter F.4 WV269 of 74 Squadron taking part in Exercise Vigilant in May 1957. This aircraft was originally delivered to 54 Squadron in June 1955. After service with 74 Squadron it was stored at 5 MU and scrapped in 1961. (*Newark Air Museum*)

Hunter F.4 WV326 first flew on 7 June 1955 and was delivered to 54 Squadron on 5 July 1955. It moved to 74 Squadron and was retired to 1 SofTT at Halton for ground training as 7669M, where it was noted in September 1970 still in 74 Squadron markings. It returned to HAL in January 1972 for conversion to FR.71A for Chile, where it was delivered on 11 January 1974. (*Philip Birtles*)

very short time; for example, 245 Squadron was equipped with the Hunter F.4 for just four months, between March and June 1957.

Some early F.4s were delivered to the AFDS and DFLS at West Raynham for the benefit of new flight and squadron commanders, ready to be assigned to units. Others were allocated to the Central Flying School (CFS). These aircraft were not fitted with underwing fuel tanks. The first three F.4s were delivered to Little Rissington on 7 November 1955 to form the Hunter Flight. With the main runway only 1,600 yards long, there were problems with overheated brakes and tyres on landing. This resulted in the move to Kemble, where the MU staff provided ground support. The role of the CFS was to provide qualified flying instructors (QFIs) to RAF Training Command, as well as the FAA, army and overseas air forces.

The first Hunter conversion course began on 12 November 1955 with four instructors converted every two days. A typical sortie was as follows: departure from Kemble and a climb to 35,000 feet, making a sonic bang over the Bristol Channel, followed by exercises in stalling, aerobatics and possibly a spin, before returning to Kemble. The Hunter Flight became 3 Squadron CFS, and was responsible for giving instructors flying experience of representative advanced service aircraft, for which the Hunter was ideal. The CFS gave the trainers a better appreciation of the problems their students would experience with modern

Hunter F.4 WW658 O of 98 Squadron, based at Jever. (*RAF Museum*)

Hunter F.4 XE665 A of 118 Squadron, *c.* 1955. (*Vic Flintham collection*)

Hunter F.4 WT748 S of 118 Squadron, RAF Germany. (*RAF Museum*)

A formation of Hunter F.4s with 14 Squadron, RAF Germany. (*RAF Museum*)

Hunter F.4 WV275 D of IV Squadron. (*BAE Systems*)

Hunter F.4 WV391 Z of 20 Squadron, *c.* 1955. (*Vic Flintham collection*)

A Hunter F.4 with 67 Squadron, 4 May 1957. (*RAF Museum*)

Hunter F.4 XF319 was delivered to 5 MU on 25 January 1956 and was initially issued to 66 Squadron on 15 March. It was then operated by 112 Squadron from 4 December 1956 until it was retired to Kemble on 17 April 1957. It moved to Halton as 7849M where it was noted in 112 Squadron markings in April 1978. It was registered as G-BTCY on 22 January 1991 but withdrawn on 10 March 1999, following which it was shipped to the USA. (*Philip Birtles*)

Hunter F.4 XF319 while in service with 112 Squadron at Brüggen. (*RAF Museum*)

A Hunter F.4 of 112 Squadron in formation with Sabre XB920 during transition to Hunters in 1956. (*RAF Museum*)

A 130 Squadron Hunter F.4 at Brüggen in 1957. (*Author's collection*)

Hunter F.4 XE718 A of 93 Squadron at Geilenkirchen in March 1956. (*RAF Museum*)

Hunter F.4 WT746 first flew on 1 March 1955 and was delivered to 5 MU on 17 March. It served with AFDS and 71 Squadron, becoming 7770M at Halton on 28 November 1962, where it was noted in April 1978 in 71 Squadron markings. It was withdrawn on 12 November 1962 and allocated to army training at Saighton Camp. It is now at the Dumfries and Galloway Aviation Museum. (*Philip Birtles*)

Hunter F.4 XF938 of 71 Squadron in Denmark, 1958. (*Vic Flintham collection*)

Hunter F.4 WV332 first flew on 7 June 1955 and was delivered to 67 Squadron on 12 March 1956. It moved to 112 Squadron on 18 April 1957 and finally operated with 234 Squadron from 6 May 1957. It was withdrawn to 5 MU and allocated to Halton for ground instruction as 7673M on 17 January 1961, where it was noted in 234 Squadron markings in March 1970. It returned to HAL in July 1972 for conversion to a T.68 for Switzerland, where it was delivered on 2 August 1974 as J-4201. The original nose is at Tangmere Aviation Museum. (*Philip Birtles*)

A Hunter F.4 of 234 Squadron, RAF Germany, in June 1957. (*RAF Museum*)

swept-wing aircraft. Training Command pilots who joined the Hunter Flight came in three categories: the first was of pilots on a QFI course—they flew three conversion sorties; the second group consisted of QFIs from the RAF Flying College at Cranwell and various other flight training schools—they flew nine sorties throughout one week; the third category consisted of CFS staff instructors who maintained their currency on type.

The Central Flying School was also responsible for the recategorisation and standardisation of Hunter QFIs and pilots. Three more F.4s joined the Hunter Flight in July 1957, and two Hunter T.7s were added in 1960, one of which was WV318, which later returned to Kemble with Delta Jets. By the end of 1960, fifty-two Training Command pilots, sixty CFS staff and forty-nine CFS students had been trained by the three staff instructors at CFS Kemble, each of whom were ex-Hunter squadron pilots, having completed a tour of instruction at a flying training school. On 28 February 1963, the swept-wing commitment was transferred to the Gnat T.1 Squadron and the two remaining F.4s were put into storage at 5 MU.

Produced at Coventry, the Hunter F.5 was powered by a Sapphire 101 turbojet and was similarly improved to the F.4 standard with wing hard points and increased internal fuel. The first F.5 was WN954, the forty-sixth off the line, which first flew on 19 October 1954, a day ahead of the first Hawker-built F.4. Deliveries started in 1955 to 1, 34, 41, 56 and 263 Squadrons in UK-based Fighter Command. Based at Tangmere, 1 Squadron began to take deliveries in September 1955, followed the next month by 34 Squadron at the same airfield. Both squadrons were posted to Nicosia in Cyprus flying escort to RAF Canberra bombers against Egyptian airfields in October 1956. No. 1 Squadron was disbanded on 1 July 1958 but reformed the next day as 263 Squadron at Stradishall, equipped with Hunter F.6s. No. 34 Squadron was disbanded on 15 January 1958, and its aircraft went to 208 Squadron. At Biggin Hill, 41 Squadron replaced its Meteor F.8s with Hunter F.5s in June 1955. The squadron was disbanded on 31 January 1958. At Waterbeach, 56 Squadron was pleased to exchange its troublesome Swifts for Hunter F.5s in May 1955, and over three years later, in November 1958, these F5s were replaced with F.6s. At Wattisham, 263 Squadron operated Hunter F.5s alongside F.2s from May 1955 to August 1956, when the squadron re-equipped with F.6s at Wymeswold. It was renumbered 1 Squadron at Stradishall on 2 July 1958.

Hunter F.5 WN955 was used as a flying test bed for the 10,000-lb-thrust Sapphire ASSa.7, an insurance against delays or development difficulties with the Avon 203, the engine allocated for the Hunter F.6. In the event, the Avon 203's development and performance progressed without any problems, so the Sapphire ASSa.7 project was cancelled. WN958 was one of only a few Hunter F.5s modified to carry underwing ground-attack weapons with rocket projectiles (RP) outboard of the drop fuel tanks.

Hunter F.4s were very much in the front line in Germany, having replaced the interim Sabres and earlier first-generation Venom fighter bombers. Each Hunter base was classified as a wing consisting of two or three squadrons.

Hunter F.1 WT680 Z of the DFLS in Iraq, 1955. (*Vic Flintham collection*)

Hunter F.4 XF973 with the CFS. (*RAF Museum*)

Hunter F.5 WP114 was used for Sapphire flight development. (*Newark Air Museum*)

The fifth production Hunter F.5, WN958, was used for RP firing trials. (*RAF Museum*)

A formal photograph of 1 Squadron at Tangmere with Hunter F.5s. WP190, on the right as 'K', joined 1 Squadron on 13 August 1955 and operated from Nicosia during the Suez Crisis. It was allocated to ground instruction as 7582M at Bircham Newton on 10 September 1958. It was restored at Hucclecote and donated to the Tangmere Aviation Museum in June 2002. (*Author's collection*)

Hunter F.5 WP199 with 1 Squadron in October 1955. (*RAF Museum*)

Hunter F.5 WP185 with 34 Squadron in 1956. (*RAF Museum*)

Hunter F.5 WP130 with 34 Squadron during the Suez campaign. (*RAF Museum*)

A fine echelon of 41 Squadron Hunter F.5s. (*Vic Flintham collection*)

No. 41 Squadron Hunter F.5s on final approach to Biggin Hill. (*RAF Museum*)

Above: Hunter F.5 WP147 was delivered to 45 MU on 13 June 1955 and was issued to 41 Squadron, later serving with 1 Squadron. (*RAF Museum*)

Left: A formation of Hunter F.5s with 41 Squadron, consisting of WP147 L, WP133 D, WN965 P, WN961 G, WP148 and WN963. (*Author's collection*)

No. 56 Squadron Hunter F.4s in Exercise Stronghold, 1956. (*Vic Flintham collection*)

No. 56 Squadron Hunter F.4s WP103, WP104, WP123 and WN976 practice formation. (*Vic Flintham collection*)

Hunter F.5 WP120 S of 56 Squadron at Mildenhall, May 1956. (*Vic Flintham collection*)

Each RAF Germany squadron maintained a two-Hunter immediate readiness battle flight, shared between the based squadrons, with the remainder of the aircraft and crews at fifteen minutes' readiness. Squadrons based at Brüggen and Geilenkirchen were allocated to the defence of the Ruhr, and Hunters based at Jever and Oldenburg were responsible for defence over the north German plains. In the case of conflict, the Hunters were to provide defence for the 2nd TAF Canberras.

Initially the Hunter F.4s were no improvement over the Sabres they replaced, particularly as they were restricted to firing guns under 25,000 feet; this was while potential Soviet bombers flew at up to twice that altitude. This restriction was removed when the Avon 121 engines were fitted. For the three Venom squadrons, the arrival of the Hunter was most welcome as it had a far superior performance. The Sabre had a better endurance and a similar top speed, but the less sophisticated Hunter was more suited to the rigours of operations in Germany. The Hunter's cartridge starting system allowed it to get airborne much quicker than the Sabre, which used an external power source for starting. As for armament, the Hunter had the advantage with its formidable four Aden 30-mm cannons against the Sabre's six 0.5-inch machine guns, which were only effective against soft-skinned targets. The Hunter was also more robust than the Sabre with clearance to 7.5-g manoeuvres, having been tested to 11.25 g to give adequate margin. As a result, the Hunter could be subjected to much rougher handling, which was vital in a potential dogfight.

The Hunter F.4 soon gained the enthusiasm of both the Venom and Sabre pilots, who found it easy to operate. Operational training continued with the aircraft going up to the combat ceiling for high-altitude interception practice directed by ground-based GCI radar systems. With its light fuel load, Hunters could easily reach 50,000 feet and cruise around until there was only sufficient fuel left to return to base. The Avon 100 series engines were prone to surging caused by the high angle of attack manoeuvres and overuse of the throttle. The cure was to dive away with wings level, followed by the other aircraft in the formation. Even with modest restrictions remaining, the Hunter F.4 proved to be a successful aircraft, and a major improvement over the Meteors and Venoms it replaced.

Then came the government's disastrous 1957 Defence White Paper, presented by Duncan Sandys, the minister of defence. One of the major edicts of this White Paper was that fighter aircraft were to be replaced by ground-to-air guided missiles. It did not seem to matter that neither these missiles, nor the technology to develop them, existed at the time. The RAF Hunter force was one of the casualties: the flying units of the RAuxAF, where earlier Hunter marks were going to be used to replace the outdated Meteors and Vampires, were disbanded in 1957. Both Fighter Command and RAF Germany were forced to disband many of the Hunter squadrons; in many cases, these squadrons were still working up to operational status. Within a year of the defence review, RAF Germany was reduced from thirteen to four squadrons, which accounts for the short operational life of many units. RAF Germany Hunters were reduced to policing duties, while Fighter Command was given responsibility for the defence of Britain's strategic V-Bomber force. The only manned fighter to remain in development was the English Electric Lightning. The retirement of the Hunter F.4s and F.5s left a serious gap in Britain's fighter defence, but fortunately Hawker was developing the much more capable Hunter F.6: the basis of the ultimate interceptor version of this classic jet fighter.

4

Mark 6:
The Ultimate Hunter Fighter

The supersonic P1083 Hunter development was abandoned due to an air staff preference for larger turbojets without reheat, instead of the higher power and fuel consumption of reheated engines. It was still possible, however, to take the basic Hunter design, with its proven attributes, and to overcome its early shortcomings. As a result, the ultimate Hunter day fighter, project number P1099, was proposed, powered by a 10,500-lb-thrust Avon 200 series turbojet. This was the Hunter F.6.

Internal fuel capacity was increased by 25 gallons via a pair of bag tanks placed adjacent to the jet pipe, plus a 200-gallon fuselage tank and a 140-gallon bag tank in each wing. In addition, provision was made for four 100-gallon underwing pylon-mounted drop tanks. For long-range ferry flight, a pair of 230-gallon drop tanks could be carried on the inboard pylons, although these interfered with the selection of full landing flaps. The improved endurance was demonstrated in October 1958 with a flight of 1,588 miles from Dunsfold to El Adem in Libya.

Using the centre fuselage section of the cancelled P1083, the prototype XF833 was designed and built without delay, and was ready for its first flight on 22 January 1954, long before the Hunter F.4s and F.5s were entering service. It was delivered to the A&AEE at Boscombe Down in February, but suffered a forced landing due to engine failure. Following repairs it was soon flying again, but once more was damaged in a forced landing due to engine failure. On investigation, it was found the Avon engine suffered compressor blade fatigue; following modifications, the thrust was reduced to 10,000 lb. Once flying started again in July 1954, the aircraft was allocated to performance, handling and gun firing development trials at Dunsfold and the establishments. Following these trials, the aircraft was delivered to Miles Aircraft for the installation of reverse thrust under contract to Rolls-Royce. In this form it was demonstrated at Farnborough in 1956 and 1957.

On 25 March 1955, just as the F.4s and F.5s were entering service with Fighter Command in the UK and the 2nd TAF in Germany, the first interim-production Hunter F.6, WW592, was flown from Dunsfold. By the end of the year, nine

Hunter F.6 prototype XF833 with Rolls-Royce after conversion to reverse engine thrust by Miles Aircraft at Shoreham, June 1956. This aircraft first flew in its original form on 22 January 1954. (*Newark Air Museum*)

Hunter F.6 prototype XF833 waiting its turn to display at the Farnborough Air Show in September 1957. (*RAFM*)

F.6s had completed at Kingston, many of which were used in development and acceptance trials with the RAF. Seven of the early aircraft were modified from F.1s as a pre-production batch to help share the early service testing. During these trials it was found that under certain conditions, when high g was applied, the aircraft tended to pitch up. Wing fences proved ineffective, but the solution was to move forward the aerodynamic centre of pressure by a dog-tooth cutout in the outer wing leading edge, reducing the thickness-chord ratio. This became standard on all Hunter F.6s, as well as a few late production F.4s.

Engine surging with the Avon 200 series persisted, and when the guns were fired at high speed, there continued to be a nose pitch down. To solve these inherent problems, Hawker undertook a programme of intensive trials during which more than 20,000 rounds were fired. Finally a solution was found with the addition of a blast deflector: although it slightly marred the smooth lines of the Hunter's nose, it cleared the blast away from the aircraft at 90 degrees and solved the problem at last.

Production was shared between Kingston, Blackpool and Coventry, but now, as Sapphire development had been cancelled, all new aircraft were powered by Avon 200 series engines. During 1956 and 1957 a further 374 Hunter F.6s were produced from the three factories, and by the end of 1956 the new Hunter had begun to enter service with Fighter Command, and shortly after that, with 2nd TAF. The improvements to the flying controls and the addition of the more powerful and reliable Avon were popular modifications among the pilots, and the type was established in service for a considerable time. Among the improvements made to flying control was, in effect, an all-flying tail: every 2 degrees of elevator movement gave a complimentary tailplane movement of 0.7 degrees per second. Any small adjustments did not trigger tailplane movement, which made control in formation aerobatics much easier.

The unreliable cartridge starting system was replaced by an Avpin liquid starting system, although Avpin was unstable and not universally available should a Hunter need to divert to an unequipped airfield. The liquid was prone to uncontrolled explosions which could cause major damage to the aircraft, and therefore it was not ideal.

The first full-production-standard Hunter F.6s were XE526 and XE527. They were delivered on 11 January 1956 to 5 MU at Kemble and 19 MU at St Athan respectively, when both MUs were still fully occupied with preparations and delivery of F.4s and F.5s to the RAF. The first unit to receive F.6s was 54 Squadron at Odiham in September 1955; the aircraft remained in service there until January 1957. After 54 Squadron, deliveries of the F.6 were made to the following units: 263 Squadron at Wymeswold in August 1956 (this squadron retained the type until it was disbanded on 2 July 1958); 19 Squadron at Church Fenton and 66 Squadron at Linton-on-Ouse in October 1956; 43 Squadron at Leuchars (replacing F.4s), 65 Squadron at Duxford (replacing Meteor F.8s), 111 Squadron at North Weald (replacing Hunter F.4s) and 63 Squadron at Waterbeach (replacing Meteor F.8s) in November 1956; 247 Squadron at Odiham in March

The second production Hunter F.6, WW593. (*RAF Museum*)

Production standard Hunter F.6, XE618. (*RAF Museum*)

1957 (until the unit was disbanded on 31 December the same year); 74 Squadron at Horsham St Faith in November 1957 (this squadron retained the type until it converted to Lightnings at Coltishall); 1 Squadron at Stradishall in July 1958, which continued to operate F.6s until March 1960; and finally, 56 Squadron in November 1958, which operated F.6s until January 1961, when it converted to Lightnings at Wattisham.

Soon after 111 Squadron began flying the Hunter F.6, it was designated as the official RAF Fighter Command display team under the leadership of Squadron Leader Roger Topp. The aircraft were painted in an overall gloss black and the team, which used all sixteen squadron aircraft, became known as the Black Arrows.

No. 111 Squadron had originally formed on 1 August 1917 at Deir-el-Bellah in Palestine with five different types of scout aircraft. Their role was to destroy enemy reconnaissance aircraft and to protect British aircraft both in the air and on the ground. The squadron was renumbered 14 Squadron at Ramleh on 1 February 1920 and then reformed at Duxford on 1 October 1923 as part of Britain's permanent fighter defence, equipped with Sopwith Snipes, Gloster Grebes and Armstrong Whitworth Siskins. The squadron moved to Northolt on 12 July 1934 and was responsible for introducing the Hawker Hurricane into RAF service from December 1937. The squadron played a major role in the Battle of Britain. In April 1941 Spitfire Is replaced the Hurricanes and the squadron progressed to Mk IXcs until it was disbanded at Treviso in Italy on 16 May 1947. It reformed at North Weald on 2 December 1953 equipped with Meteor F.8s, which were replaced by Hunter F.4s from June 1955 until November 1956, when the Hunter F.6 arrived.

Squadron Leader Roger Topp had flown with the Glider Pilot Regiment during Operation Varsity, the Rhine crossing in March 1945, and had served with a number of RAF Germany Mosquito squadrons after the war, when he was awarded the AFC. Between 1950 and 1954 he was a staff pilot at RAE Farnborough. He flew with John Cunningham in Comet I as part of the investigation into the accidents, checking for uncontrolled flutter, following which he was awarded a bar to his AFC.

Having flown a number of different types during his tour at Farnborough, Topp found returning to routine squadron life dull. To create some excitement, he took over the leadership of a three-strong Meteor aerobatic team. The team did not perform public displays, but with the addition of a fourth aircraft, the practice in aerobatics became an efficient way for the squadron's pilots to gain experience in formation flying. When the Hunter arrived, the team completed six of the ten conversion exercises before resuming aerobatics on 15 July 1955. They had only six more practices in the Hunter before giving a display at the annual inspection by the AOC at North Weald on 22 July. All aerobatic team practices and presentations were in addition to normal operational training. Squadron Leader Topp gained publicity by establishing a new Edinburgh-to-London speed record, flying Hunter WT739 at an average speed of 717.5 mph in August 1955,

Hunter F.6 XF420 K of 54 Squadron. (*J. J. Halley*)

No. 54 Squadron Hunter F.6 XG261 at Brüggen in April 1957. (*RAF Museum*)

Hunter F.6 XE584 with 263 Squadron at Shepherds Grove on 17 May 1958. This aircraft was delivered to 19 MU on 10 April 1956 and was flown by the CFE, DFLS and 53 Squadron before being issued to Stradishall-based 263 Squadron. It then went to 1 Squadron before conversion to an interim FGA.9 with the Avon 203. It was briefly issued to 208 Squadron, followed by 8 Squadron and 229 OCU before returning to HSA in February 1976, from where it was disposed in 1979. The nose section is with the North-West Aviation Heritage Museum at Hooton Park. (*Newark Air Museum*)

Hunter F.6 XF449 of 19 Squadron served originally with 263 Squadron before going to 19 Squadron at Church Fenton in 1957. It then passed to 92 Squadron, where it became part of the Blue Diamonds aerobatic team. It was then passed to the CFE. It caught fire while taxiing at Binbrook on 6 June 1963, and was damaged beyond repair. (*Author's collection*)

Hunter F.6 XG172 of 19 Squadron was delivered to 5 MU on 19 September 1956. After service with 19 Squadron it went to 263 Squadron and 229 OCU. It moved to Brawdy with 1 TWU in October 1976 and was later issued to ground training at Scampton as 8832M. It is preserved with the City of Norwich Aviation Museum, marked as XG168. (*J. J. Halley*)

Hunter F.6 XG255 S of 66 Squadron at Akrotiri. (*Vic Flintham collection*)

Hunter F.6s with 43 Squadron over Cyprus in April 1960. (*RAF Museum*)

Hunter F.6 XF507 of 65 Squadron at Duxford. It was originally delivered to 66 Squadron in October 1956 and then went to 65 Squadron on 28 November of the same year. It was written off in a crash near Thrapston, Northants, on 30 May 1960. (*Newark Air Museum*)

Hunter F.6 XF507 with 54 Squadron. (*RAF Museum*)

A close up of the 65 Squadron badge on the nose of a Hunter F.6 H at Duxford. The picture shows the aircraft's 30-mm cannon-blast deflectors. (*J. J. Halley*)

A Hunter F.6 with 63 Squadron at Waterbeach in 1956. (*Vic Flintham collection*)

Hunter F.6s with 247 Squadron at Odiham in 1959. (*RAF Museum*)

Hunter F.6 XF504 of 74 Squadron was converted to Rhodesian FGA.9 125 and delivered to Thornhill on 19 April 1963. (*RAF Museum*)

Hunter F.6 XG159 with 56 Squadron at West Malling in 1960. (*RAF Museum*)

Hunter F.6 XG203 of 111 Squadron 'Black Arrows' was delivered to 5 MU on 17 October 1956 and was first operated by 43 Squadron. On 30 April 1957 it bounced on landing at North Weald and cartwheeled before exploding. The aircraft was a write-off but the pilot survived when he involuntarily ejected sideways. (*Newark Air Museum*)

beating the previous record set by 111 Squadron CO Squadron Leader John Gillan in Hurricane L1555 on 10 February 1938. Gillan had achieved an average speed of 408.75 mph, with the benefit of an 80-mph tailwind.

One of the original aerobatic team members was Flight Lieutenant George Aird, who later became a test pilot for the de Havilland Propeller Company at Hatfield, flying Sea Vixens and Lightnings on Firestreak and assisting with Red Top air-to-air missile development. Aird won dubious claim to fame by ejecting from Lightning F.1 XG332 on 13 September 1962 on finals at Hatfield Aerodrome. There was insufficient time for the parachute to deploy and Aird landed in a greenhouse full of tomatoes. The greenhouse broke his fall, though he suffered from two broken legs and other injuries. He made a full recovery, however, and was flying Lightnings again a year later, although he had lost an inch or so in height.

Roger Topp exploited the improved performance of the Hunter F.4s by forming a four-aircraft team in March 1956. On 23 April he was nominated to represent 11 Group Fighter Command in the Midlands and southern England. Their opening display was at Bordeaux for the French National Air Display on 12 May. This was followed by the Zurich International Air Display where some half a million people attended. Returning to Britain, Topp and his team performed at the RAFA display at Sydenham, Belfast, in June, and at Odiham in July for the state visit to Britain of King Feisal of Iraq.

As the season progressed and his confidence grew, Squadron Leader Topp considered increasing his team to five aircraft to differentiate it from the other international teams. He concentrated on remaining in public view during his displays, unlike some of the full-time 'professional' teams, which could be out of sight of the audience for over a minute. Approval was given in August to add the fifth Hunter, which appeared in public for the first time at the Battle of Britain displays at Biggin Hill and West Malling in September to close its season. After flying nine shows in its first full season, 'Treble One' Squadron was nominated as Fighter Command's leading aerobatic team for 1957 by the AOC-in-C, Air Chief Marshal Sir Thomas Pike.

Training for the new season began in January 1957, with the new Hunter F.6s having replaced the earlier aircraft in November 1956. With approval as the RAF's premier aerobatic team, permission was given for the standard camouflage finish to be replaced by special display colours. After discussions with squadron members, an overall gloss black scheme was chosen to portray the squadron colours and give high visibility for public displays. The first aircraft to be painted in the new scheme was F.6 XG201, and soon afterwards the standard fin flash was restored with red serial numbers. The Union Jack was painted on the starboard side of the nose, and the black squadron bars either side of the fuselage roundel were outlined in gold lines.

The display season started on 26 March with a five-Hunter display at Leuchars to celebrate the presentation of 43 Squadron Standard, followed by the presentation of 111 Squadron Standard at North Weald on 30 April by Air Chief Marshal Sir Harry Broadhurst. Unfortunately the last aircraft to land bounced heavily and disintegrated, catching fire, although the pilot managed to escape serious injury when his ejection seat inadvertently threw him clear of the aircraft. He recovered in time to return to the squadron in July.

During the 1956 display season, experiments had been made with smoke generation, but it was not until the 1957 season that smoke was produced by installing a diesel tank in the ammunition bay. The first international air display in 1957 was the Paris Air Show in June, and a keen rivalry was felt between the four international teams. Initially, Treble One Squadron was the only team with five aircraft, but the other teams copied them by introducing their reserve as a fifth aircraft. To beat the competition, Roger Topp added his two reserves making a formation of seven, with the reserves filling in the slots in front of the crowd while the main formation changed positions. The team had no official name at this stage, but a comment in the French newspaper *Le Figaro* referred to the British team as 'les Flèches Noir', which translates as 'the Black Arrows': it was the name adopted by Roger Topp.

In September, the Black Arrows featured nine Hunters at the Farnborough Air Show, opening with a perfect loop and roll before the formation split up for the regular five-aircraft performance. Later the same month, the Black Arrows were pitted against the USAF Skyblazers at the Biggin Hill Battle of Britain Air Show. The American team flew rigid precise formations with a great deal of noise, but the Black Arrows were preferred due to their constant changing of formation and use of smoke. When the Skyblazers adopted smoke, the fin and rudder of the box aircraft was painted black in an effort to demonstrate how close they formated.

On 19 February 1958, with North Weald approaching closure as an RAF airfield, 111 Squadron was detached temporarily to North Luffenham.

Nine Hunters of the 111 Squadron 'Black Arrows' during formation practice in 1962. (*RAF Museum*)

A Black Arrows display at Farnborough. (*BAE Systems*)

A tight formation of five Black Arrows Hunter F.6s. (*BAE Systems*)

Preparations, including runway resurfacing, were made at Wattisham, meanwhile, to receive the squadron. These were completed on 18 June.

To maintain the high standards expected of Fighter Command's premier aerobatic team, new formations and manoeuvres were being created on a regular basis, and Roger Topp was determined to make a major impression at the 1958 Farnborough Air Show. Working closely with the AOC-in-C Fighter Command, Air Chief Marshal Sir Thomas Pike, from whom he enjoyed full support, Topp conceived a plan to make a mass formation loop as the show finale. The loop to beat was one made by the Pakistan Air Force, which had used sixteen F-86 Sabres in February 1957 in honour of a state visit by the king of Afghanistan. The Black Arrows' total compliment was sixteen Hunters, but to achieve a greater impact more aircraft and pilots were needed. The original plan was to fly twenty aircraft in the formation, with guest pilots flying a less demanding line, astern position. With five in the leading 'vic', four in line astern proved to be too many and created difficulties for pilots in maintaining position in the loop. The alternative was three vics of seven aircraft which was difficult to fly, but more effective. This brought the total to twenty-one Hunters with an extra aircraft on the rear centre line to make twenty-two.

To avoid depleting front-line strength, the additional Hunters were added initially from Command Reserve. The additional volunteers, on detachment to 111 Squadron until after the Farnborough Air Show, began to arrive in July 1958 and were assessed before going through an intensive training regime in gradually increasing formation sizes. Going over the top of the loop was the most demanding part, with the leader accelerating down while the tail end aircraft were still climbing. The answer was for the leader to relax the 'g' for a short while when he was inverted, until the tail end aircraft caught up, and then to pull more 'g' on the way down as the other aircraft regained position. Fourteen of the Hunters were in the black 111 Squadron colours while the other eight were in standard RAF Fighter Command camouflage. On 12 August the world record of twenty-one aircraft was achieved and ten days later the full twenty-two aircraft were looped. Based at Odiham, the twenty-two-aircraft formation was flown twice daily from 25 August, ready for the start of the show week from 1 to 7 September. At the Farnborough display, an initial loop was performed by twenty-two Hunters, followed by a second loop with sixteen aircraft, which then rolled in formation. With seven leaving the formation, the remaining nine looped, with four more breaking away for a bomb-burst, leaving five Hunters to finish the show.

A repeat performance with twenty-two Hunters looping was flown twice at Wattisham on 11 September, the second time for the AOC-in-C. The twenty-eighth and final display of the season was a nine-aircraft show two weeks later for the ROC at Odiham. The twenty-two-Hunter formation was a finale for Roger Topp, who after leading the team for two years was promoted and posted to a ground task at HQ Allied Air Forces Central Europe. He went on to command the Fighter Test Squadron at Boscombe Down and completed his RAF career as station commander at Coltishall.

Roger Topp was succeeded as CO and team leader of the Black Arrows in October 1958 by Squadron Leader Peter Latham. At this point only seven of the original Treble One pilots remained on the squadron. With insufficient seniority to take command among the remaining pilots, Peter Latham was posted in for the demanding role of continuing to develop the Black Arrows after such a major achievement. Latham began aerobatic flying with experienced flyers such as Brian Mercer and Paddy Hine, building up a mutual confidence within the team. As a squadron CO, Latham had to maintain authoritarian control, but within the aerobatic team he was an equal member of the team.

The nine-aircraft team was used for the 1959 season in developing new formations, including 'wine glass,' 'voodoo' and 'big cross', designed to best display the team's flying skills. This effort to align the show for the spectators was an innovation in the way formation aerobatics were presented. The squadron began the 1959 season with nine-aircraft formations as standard, but for the major international air shows at Paris and Farnborough, the team split into two parts consisting of sixteen aircraft in total, with a co-ordinated programme: one of nine aircraft led by Peter Latham and the other of seven aircraft led by Flight Lieutenant Brian Mercer, who had joined the squadron in December 1957. The display was reduced to ten minutes and allowed an increased number of manoeuvres.

A total of fifty-five displays were flown by the Black Arrows in 1959, and with the growing international demand to see the team in 1960, bookings were made in France, Germany and Spain. A tour of the USA planned for autumn of 1960 had to be cancelled due to operational commitments. In March 1960, HRH the duke of Edinburgh presented the Royal Aero Club Britannia Challenge Trophy for the Black Arrows' achievements during the 1959 season. The final Farnborough appearance

The famous twenty-two-Hunter loop by the Black Arrows. (*BAE Systems*)

Squadron Leader Roger Topp flying Hunter F.6 XG194 during the Farnborough Air Show in September 1958. (*RAF Museum*)

in September 1960 started with a pterodactyl loop by eighteen aircraft. This premier show was followed by Battle of Britain shows at Gaydon, Coltishall, Biggin Hill and Wattisham, and then by displays at Brüggen and Barcelona, completing the season. After this the squadron was stood down as Fighter Command's premier display team in order to prepare for conversion to the Lightning.

With such high standards of formation jet-fighter aerobatics set internationally by the Black Arrows, the RAF could not bow out of presenting displays in national and international shows.

In March 1957, 92 Squadron began to receive F.6s at Middleton St George to replace its F.4s, and in November 1959 this squadron was nominated as the RAF's official reserve aerobatic team, giving ten shows between May and September 1960. To replace Treble One was going to be a challenge, but the Hunter was the ideal platform, despite its limited operational life with the Lightning's entry into service. There was wide speculation that 92 Squadron would be selected as the RAF's premier aerobatic team, and even more so when, in October 1960, Squadron Leader Brian Mercer appointed as CO. He immediately started the process of selecting candidates for the new aerobatic team. Despite its previous performance as the reserve team, the AOC-in-C Fighter Command had to be sure the squadron was capable of maintaining the high standards expected of an RAF team. The team was to fly nine Hunter F.6s, and among the pilots selected were four from 111 Squadron. In January 1961 the squadron was detached to Cyprus for nine weeks of tactical and weapons training, with the first month based at Nicosia.

A move was made to Akrotiri where, during the first three weeks, there was intensive formation aerobatics training, flying 738 sorties. By making moves that would be most appreciated by the audience, Brian Mercer intended to improve

Hunter F.6 XG228 of 92 Squadron was delivered to 5 MU on 25 October 1956. It was converted to an FGA.9 in 1965, serving with 229 OCU, 1 TWU and 79 Squadron in October 1976. (*Newark Air Museum*)

Line-up of eight 92 Squadron Hunter F.6s at Middleton St George, with a T.7 at the far end. (*RAF Museum*)

Squadron Leader R. H. B. Dixon was CO of 92 Squadron at Middleton St George from October 1958 to October 1960. (*RAF Museum*)

on what had been considered the absolute limit reached by the Black Arrows. Each display would consist of the well-tried loops, rolls, wing-overs and turns, all presented in changing formations. While the squadron was based in Cyprus, Hunters being ferried from the UK featured an attractive Royal Blue colour scheme, which had been selected by Brian Mercer. The squadron returned to Middleton St George on 10 March and approval was gained on 27 April for 92 Squadron to become the RAF's premier aerobatic team.

No. 92 Squadron had originally formed at London Colney, near St Albans, on 1 September 1917, equipped with SE.5as. It moved to France in July 1918, and after the First World War, served with the army of occupation, disbanding on 7 August 1919. The squadron reformed at Tangmere on 10 October 1939, initially equipped with Blenheim IFs, which were replaced with Spitfire Is. It became operational on 9 May 1940. During the Battle of Britain the squadron was based at Biggin Hill, and had claimed 127 victories by the end of the year. The squadron moved to Egypt in early 1942, and then to several places around the Mediterranean theatre. It continued to operate later marks of Spitfire until December 1946, when it was disbanded. The squadron reformed at Acklington on 31 January 1947 equipped with Meteor F.3s, followed by F.4s and F.8s. In January 1954, at Linton-on-Ouse, it became one of the UK-based F-86 Sabre squadrons, converting to Hunter F.4s in April 1956 when still at Linton, but then moving to Middleton St George in March 1957, equipped with F.6s.

Following an appearance at Wildenrath on 22 April 1961, a suggested title of 'Blaue Diamanten' was printed in a local newspaper, and the name 'Blue Diamonds' was adopted. With the display season getting under way, the squadron moved to Leconfield, its new base, on 26 May. There followed displays in Britain, Norway and Germany, but it was Brian Mercer's ambition to fly with sixteen Hunters. The formation was increased from nine to twelve from May, and in preparation for the Farnborough Air Show, the first sixteen-aircraft formations were flown from 18 July. A loop was started with four separate boxes of four aircraft, which joined into a diamond sixteen on the way down. Following was a series of rolls and loops with sixteen aircraft with a final break into four boxes of four, ending in all four boxes performing opposing bomb-bursts. Operating from nearby Dunsfold for the Farnborough Air Show, the first few days were limited by low cloud, but on 16 September there were displays at Battle of Britain shows at Gaydon, Biggin Hill and Waterbeach. In late September there was a brief return to operational training, ready for a tour of the Near and Middle East. The squadron left Leconfield on 12 October. Displays were flown in Cyprus, Tehran for the Iranian Air Forces Day, and the final show was in Athens with a nine-aircraft display on 23 October, completing the 1961 display season.

For the 1962 season, the Air Ministry considered replacing the Hunter with the more modern Lightning. No. 74 Squadron was nominated as the RAF's premier aerobatic team, but 92 Squadron was considered to perform a synchronised display for the Farnborough Air Show in September. Although most of the experienced display pilots had been posted for conversion to Lightnings,

92 Squadron's impressive record under Brian Mercer made the Blue Diamonds an obvious choice.

At the end of June, with just over two months before the Farnborough Air Show, the Air Ministry ordered the creation of a spectacular aerobatic display. Brian Mercer decided to revive the sixteen-Hunter formation, and he requested a number of experienced pilots to join the team, together with some new pilots. The team flew three displays during July and moved to Coltishall on 9 August to work with 74 Squadron's Lightning pilots to achieve an integrated routine. The combined formations consisted of a diamond sixteen of Hunters and a vic seven of Lightnings. Following approval by senior RAF officers, the teams moved to Farnborough on 30 August, ready for the week of displays.

In addition to the Hunters and Lightnings, the RAF had also approved displays from the Red Pelicans of the CFS, flying Jet Provosts, and the Sea Vixen and Scimitar teams of the FAA. The combined displays of the Hunters and Lightnings were to be the finales for the last two public days of the show. The SBAC Flying Committee, the secretary of state for air and the C-in-C Fighter Command were all highly in favour of the programme.

Weather conditions were poor at Farnborough, but the show started with a solo display by Dougie Bridson, who made a slow flypast, then a fast flypast and a vertical climb while performing a series of rolls. The main formation then approached in four box fours, pulling up from low level into a loop. The display continued with looping and turning while changing formation. There were upward and downward bomb bursts with a 'thread the needle' as the finale, in which four Hunters made a crossover from different directions. The team of nineteen aircraft, which included two flying reserves, flew over the airfield in echelon before breaking for downwind and landing.

Such was the popularity of the team that more requests were received than could be performed. This resulted in the formation of a second team. The Battle of Britain displays at Biggin Hill and Waterbeach were flown by the full sixteen aircraft, and then they split into two teams for Finningley and Waddington with Squadron Leader 'Paddy' Hine leading the second team. The final show for the Blue Diamonds, after two years of displays, was held on 13 October 1962 for the benefit of the AOC at Middleton St George. Following this, the team was disbanded and the pilots returned to their full-time squadron duties. In April 1963, 92 Squadron began to re-equip with Lightning F.2s and all the blue Hunters had been withdrawn by July 1963.

With the entry into service of the Hunter F.6, the majority of the earlier versions were retired. This included all of the Sapphire-powered aircraft, even though their performance was not much inferior to that of the F.6. Logistically, however, it was sensible to retire the remaining F.2s and F.5s from service.

In addition to the UK-based fighter squadrons, Hunter F.6s were delivered to RAF Germany, with IV and 93 Squadron at Jever re-equipping in February and March 1957, followed by 14 and 20 Squadrons at Oldenburg in April and May. In June 1958, when it was realised that the RAF could no longer fulfil its

No. 92 Squadron 'Blue Diamonds' Hunter F.6s lined up ready for a Farnborough Air Show with Spitfire Vb AB910 of BBMF. (*RAF Museum*)

The Blue Diamonds performing at Hucknall. (*Newark Air Museum*)

commitments to NATO, 26 Squadron re-equipped at Ahlhorn. The squadron was also issued with F.6s from the other RAF Germany squadrons, which meant that the total aircraft deployed remained the same. The F.6s delivered to Germany arrived in various states of modification, many without the dog-tooth wing leading edges and gun-blast deflectors which had to be brought up to standard at MUs. With its increased engine thrust and little improvement in internal fuel capacity, the F.6s had to carry 100-gallon drop tanks as standard, when stocks were available. No. 208 Squadron operated F.6s at Nicosia in Cyprus for a year from 1 March 1958 until 31 March 1959.

The 1957 Defence White Paper brought an immediate halt to Hunter F.6 production, leaving a total of 296 aircraft built at Kingston and 119 at Coventry. Fortunately, interest in the type was growing overseas, and orders for 128 Hunters were received from India and 100 from Switzerland. Hawker was also looking at making improvements, particularly with the carriage of weapons for the ground-attack role. Rather than being a disaster for Hawker, the Defence White Paper stimulated a wider appeal for the aircraft within the RAF and among export customers. The Lightning, meanwhile, which was the only new programme to survive the White Paper, had a greatly improved performance over the Hunter as an interceptor, but it suffered development delays to its service entry. This allowed the robust and manoeuvrable Hunter F.6 to remain in the RAF front line well into the 1960s, maintaining an acceptable capability.

Hunter F.6 XK149 of 14 Squadron was delivered to 5 MU on 26 September 1957 and initially operated with the AFDS on a tactical evaluation in 1958. After service with 14 Squadron at Gutersloh in 1962, it was operated by 1 and 54 Squadrons before going to 229 OCU with the markings of 79 Squadron. It moved to 1 TWU at Brawdy in October 1976 and was allocated to ground instruction at Cranwell as 8714M in October 1985. (*Newark Air Museum*)

Hunter F.6 XF508 with 20 Squadron at Korat in Thailand. (*RAF Museum*)

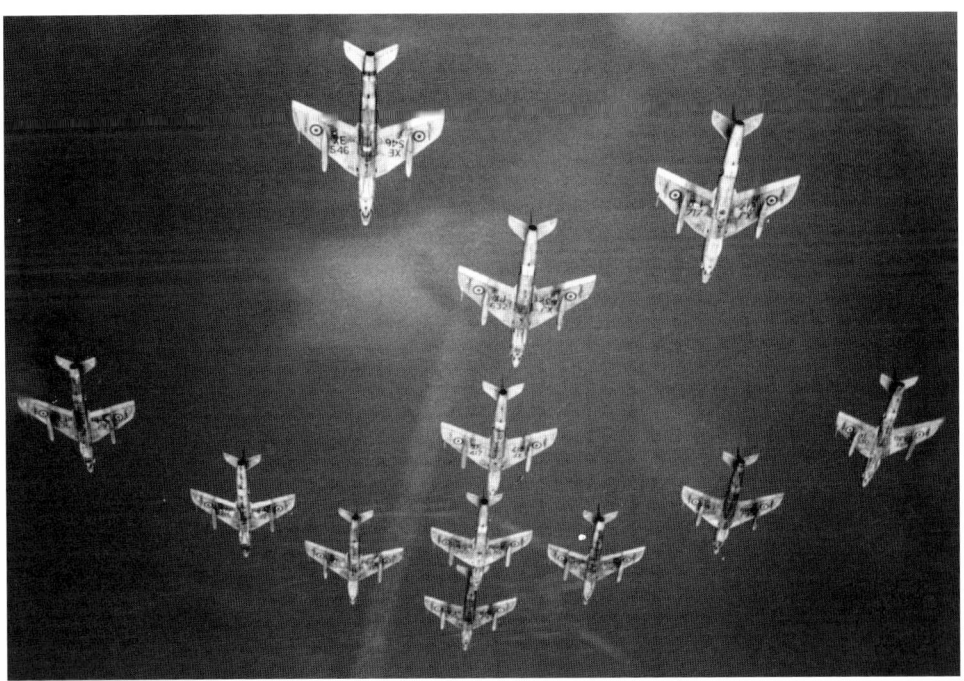

A 26 Squadron Hunter F.6 formation *en route* to Sylt. (*Vic Flintham collection*)

Hunter F.6 XE530 A of 26 Squadron, *c.* 1960. (*Vic Flintham collection*)

Hunter F.6 XF389, armed with underwing RP. This aircraft operated with 92 and 56 Squadrons, followed by West Raynham-based DFLS and DFCS. It then went to 229 OCU and was returned to HSA in May 1968 for conversion to FGA73A for Jordan, where it was delivered as 829 on 19 May 1969. (*BAE Systems*)

A formation of Tangmere-based 208 Squadron Hunter F.6s, including XF432 E, XF441 P, XE580 F and D, 1956. (*Vic Flintham collection*)

An echelon of 208 Squadron Hunter F.6s, including XF432 E and XE580 F and C. (*BAE Systems*)

No. 229 OCU at Chivenor replaced their earlier Hunters with F.6s in the 1960s. The aircraft served with 63, 79 and 234 Shadow Squadrons, with some staying long enough to move to TWU at Brawdy from 2 September 1974. The F.6s were also supplemented by FGA.9s from 1969.

With the withdrawal of the Hunter from front-line service, a surplus of robust high-performance aircraft were available for other roles like advanced pilot training. A fleet of Hunters, including T.7s and F.6s, was allocated to 4 FTS at Valley, where the aircraft were officially used for the training of overseas students, while RAF pilots were instructed in the Gnat Trainer. As the Gnat was such a tight fit for many pilots, some were posted to the Hunter, together with a number of other pilots who were able to select their aircraft of choice. The T.7s were used for conversion and basic handling instruction, but much of the instruction was carried out in the F.6s, which, with the armament removed, was fast and manoeuvrable and very popular. The aircraft also looked very smart in a high-visibility red-and-white scheme, having originally been painted in the standard camouflage finish with individual black numbers in a white circle.

Hunter F.6s also operated with the establishments, particularly XE601, which operated at A&AEE Boscombe Down for many years and was a regular visitor to air show static displays. F.6 XG290 served with Aero Flight at RAE Bedford, fitted with a long nose probe. F.6 XF378, designated P1109B, was used for de Havilland Firestreak development, carrying a missile under each wing, and was fitted with an AI.20 radar in the nose with forward facing camera fairings in place of the gun-pack. F.6A XG210 was used by Hawker Siddeley Dynamics at Hatfield for SRAAM air-to-air missile development.

NATO participants flying over Chivenor at the air show in August 1969, led by a Hunter F.6. (*Author's collection*)

A formation of the six types of aircraft operated by 229 OCU fly over the annual Chivenor air show in August 1969. Leading is a 79 Squadron F.6, followed by a Meteor F.8 and T.7, with a Hunter T.7 in the box, and a Hunter FR.10 and FGA.9 bringing up the rear. (*Philip Birtles*)

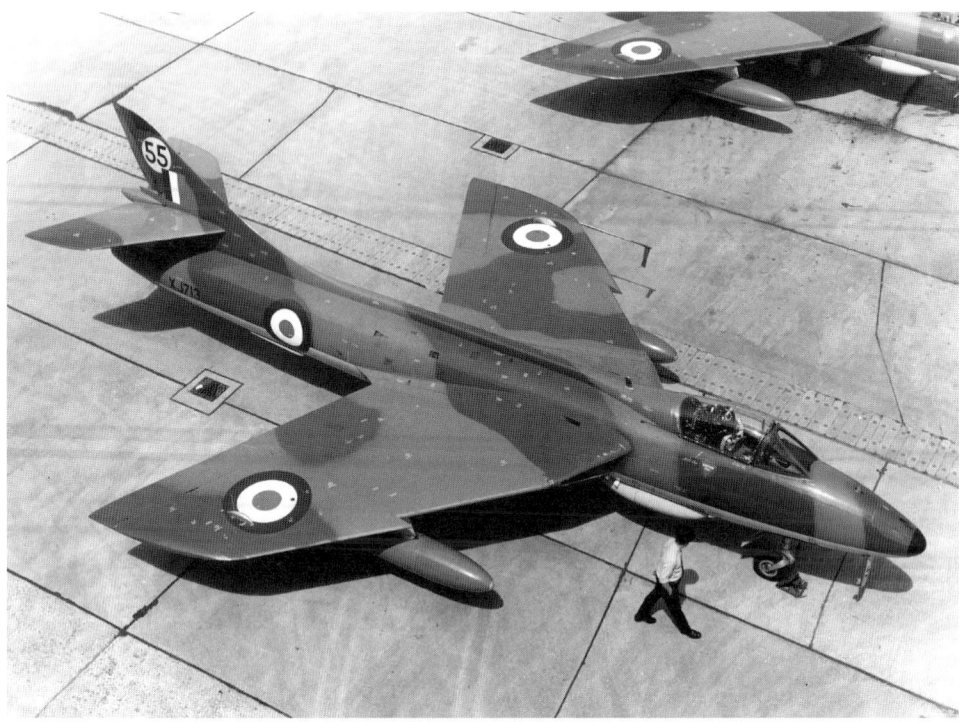

Hunter F.6 XJ713 of 229 OCU at Hatfield Open Day in July 1968 was delivered to 5 MU in May 1957 and flew with 20, 14 and 1 Squadrons before joining 229 OCU. It returned to HSA on 10 September 1969 for conversion to Chilean FGA.71 as 722, where it was delivered on 21 December 1970. It is now preserved in the Chilean Air Force Museum at Los Cerrillos. (*Philip Birtles*)

Hunter F.6 XF383 in 145 Squadron markings was with 229 OCU when at Alconbury in June 1961. It originally served with 263, 111 and 65 Squadrons before joining 229 OCU. It also flew with 12 Squadron in 1984. It was allocated to ground instruction at Wittering as 8706M and its nose is preserved at Kidlington. (*Newark Air Museum*)

Hunter F.6 XG199 of 229 OCU in 63 Squadron markings is photographed among the Hunters taking off for the massed formation flyover at the Chivenor annual air show in August 1969. This aircraft was delivered to 33 MU at Lyneham on 2 October 1956 and operated with 19 Squadron before going to 229 OCU in March 1964. It returned to HSA in December 1969 for conversion to Chilean FGA.71 as 724, where it was delivered on 18 February 1971. It is preserved at the museum at Los Cerrillos in Santiago. (*Philip Birtles*)

Hunter F.6 XG160 of 229 OCU and 79 Squadron at Greenham Common in July 1973. Built at Coventry, it was delivered to 5 MU and served with 43 Squadron and the 111 Squadron 'Black Arrows' before joining 229 OCU. It moved to 1 TWU in October 1976 and was allocated to ground instruction at Scampton as 8831M. It was auctioned in December 1994 and was acquired by the Royal Jordanian Historic Flight at Bournemouth Airport as G-BWAF. (*Philip Birtles*)

Hunter F.6 XE591 of 229 OCU and 234 Squadron with white spine at Chivenor air show in August 1964. This aircraft was delivered to 33 MU and served with 74 and 65 Squadrons before going to 229 OCU. It returned to HSA in April 1966 for conversion to Saudi Arabian F.60 60/602, and was delivered on 2 May 1966. (*Philip Birtles*)

Hunter F.6 XE656 of TWU 63 Squadron at Abingdon in September 1978. This Hunter was delivered to 19 MU on 24 August 1956 and served with 65 and 92 Squadrons, as well as the DFLS before joining 229 OCU. After service with 1 TWU it was allocated to ground instruction as 8678M and was acquired by the Auto & Technik Museum at Speyer, Germany, in 1998. (*Philip Birtles*)

Hunter F.6 XF384 with 4 FTS still in camouflage at Upper Heyford in June 1969. This Hunter was delivered to 66 Squadron on 13 September 1956, but five days later it joined 92 Squadron. Following this it went to 111 Squadron and then to West Raynham to serve with the DFLS and DFCS. It then joined 229 OCU, and after a period of storage at 5 MU, went to 4 FTS at Valley from March 1967. It had a mid-air collision with XF387 on approach to Valley on 10 August 1972, and after that it was written off and relegated to the fire dump. (*Philip Birtles*)

Hunter F.6 XG185 at Bentwaters in the high-visibility red and white markings of 4 FTS, based at Valley. This aircraft was delivered to 19 MU on 3 October 1956 and served with 3 and 19 Squadrons before going back to Kemble for storage in 1966/67. It was issued to 4 FTS in 1976, but was written off in a crash at Maltreath Sands, Anglesey, on 21 April 1976. (*Philip Birtles*)

Hunter F.6 XE601 at Boscombe Down on the celebration of the fiftieth anniversary of the A&AEE. It is pictured in the standard day-fighter camouflage finish, carrying an underwing SNEB rocket pack. The aircraft was involved in a range of trials with 'A' Squadron. (*Philip Birtles*)

Hunter F.6A XE601 with its camouflage replaced by red and grey colours. (*Newark Air Museum*)

A&AEE Hunter F6A XE601 at Fairford in July 1995. The white underwing tank was used for biological warfare spraying tests. The fate of this Hunter recounted in Chapter 9. (*Philip Birtles*)

Hunter F.6 XG290 fitted with a nose probe on the apron with Aero Flight at RAE Bedford. This F.6 was delivered to 19 MU on 18 December 1956 and served with Laarbruch Station Flight from May to October 1980. It was used at Bedford for various trials before being allocated to ground training at Halton as 8711M. It was eventually dismantled for spares support with Delta Jets at Kemble. (*Philip Birtles*)

A Hunter F.6 trials aircraft for the Fairey Fireflash air-to-air missile. (*RAF Museum*)

Hunter XF378, with the designation P1109B, was used for Firestreak development and was fitted with AI.20 radar in the nose and forward-facing cameras in the shell-case fairings. (*Newark Air Museum*)

P1109B Hunter F.6 XF378 taking off at a Farnborough Air Show with test Firestreaks under the wings and AI.20 radar in the lengthened nose. (*Author's collection*)

Hunter F.6 XF378, which was used for trialling the de Havilland Firestreak infrared heat-seeking air-to-air missiles. (*RAF Museum*)

A&AEE's Hunter F.6 fleet, which was used for weapons development. XF310 is included in the photograph. (*RAF Museum*)

Oppoite above: Hunter F.6 XK161, which was used for trials with ground-attack RP development. (*RAF Museum*)

Oppoite below: Hunter F6A XG210 was based at Hatfield for SRAAM missile development with Hawker Siddeley Dynamics and retained its camouflage finish. (*Philip Birtles*)

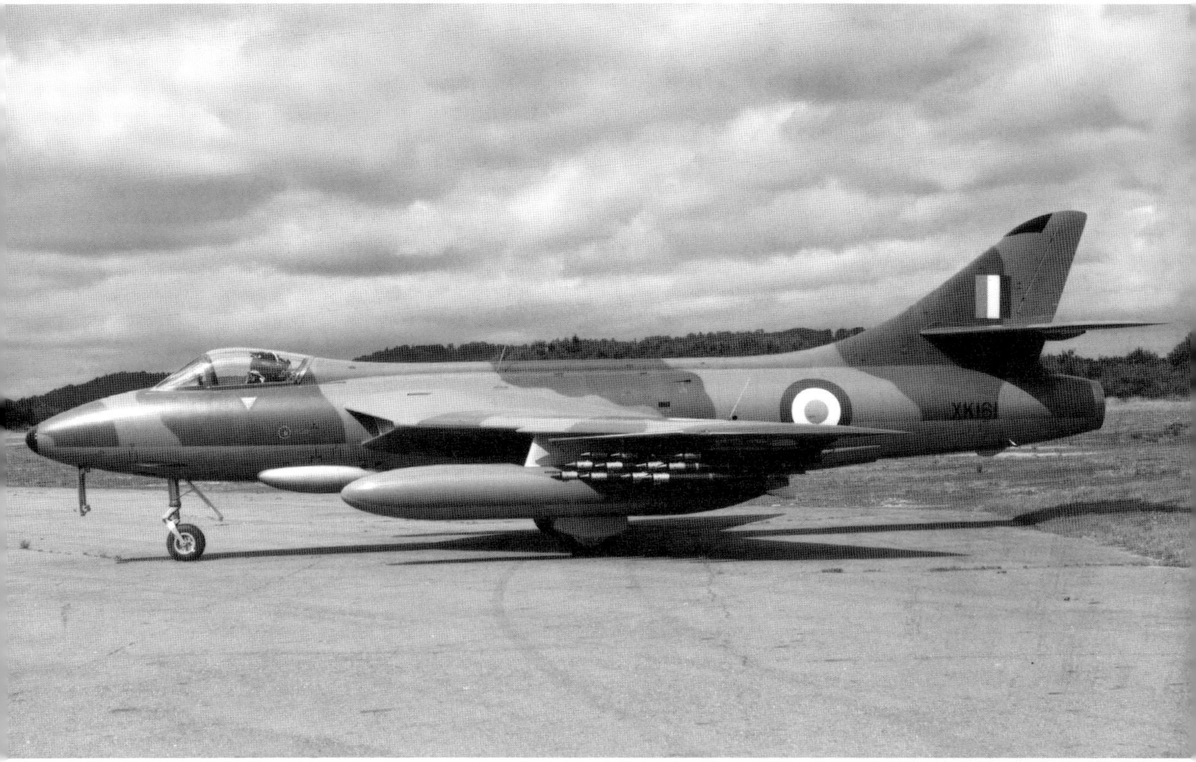
XK161

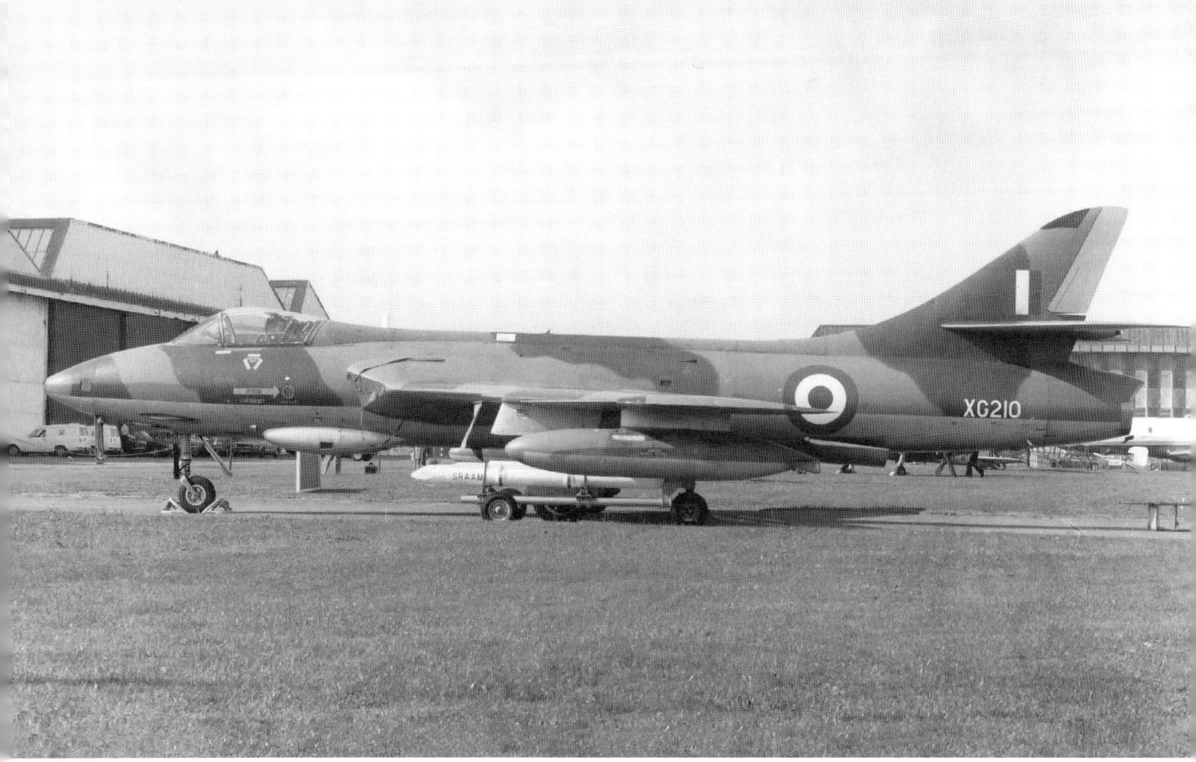
XG210

Hunter F.6A XG210 at Hatfield in September 1981, used for SRAAM air-to-air weapons development. This aircraft was originally delivered to 33 MU on 1 November 1956 and served with 66, 14 and 19 Squadrons before going to the CFE. It was then based at Cranfield, Hatfield and Bedford. It was repainted in A&AEE colours as part of the CA fleet when it returned to Hatfield for air-to-air missile development. It is now with a private collector at Beck Row, near Mildenhall—see preserved Hunters. (*Philip Birtles*)

Hunter F.6 at Dunsfold with a range of weapons which could be carried, together with fuel tanks. (*BAE Systems*)

5

Two-Seat Hunters

During the Second World War, pilots who were to fly Hurricanes and Spitfires, and later, Typhoons and Tempests, did not have the benefit of flying a conversion-training version of these types. This situation continued into the jet age with the introduction of the Vampire and Meteor, despite a high level of accidents, in particular with Meteors. Training versions were eventually ordered for both types, not so much for conversion to type, but as advanced trainers in preparation for flying the new jet fighters coming into service with Fighter Command. The main stimulus for Hawker to design a trainer version of the Hunter was the potential it had for exports, which would require conversion to type in countries without jet-fighter experience. The RAF also showed some interest in the Hunter as an advanced trainer. When squadrons experienced transition from first generation jets to early Hunters, it was not as simple as expected, so the value of the two-seat Hunter was appreciated for conversion to type.

Although design work on a two-seat version of the Hunter, dedicated for training, started in the 1950s, fighter development took priority. For experienced RAF pilots the Hunter was not too demanding to master, but the two-seat version was useful not only for pilot conversion training, but also for systems training and development. In 1953, the future Hunter T.7 was given the project designation P1101; it was started as a private venture with both tandem and side-by-side seating configurations being considered. The RAF had experience of a two-seat tandem cockpit layout with the Meteor T.7 and side-by-side with the Vampire T.11. Although the tandem layout was believed to better develop a single-seat mentality, the side-by-side was found to be more effective for weapons training and instrument flying. It was also possible for the instructor to better demonstrate and explain techniques to students.

With the issue of Specification T.157D in 1954, Hawker responded with a side-by-side configuration, and a prototype was then ordered. With the Hunter modular construction, the two-seat version featured a new forward fuselage replacing the single-pilot nose of the Hunter F.4, powered by an Avon RA.21. XJ615, the first prototype, flew on 8 July 1955.

A wooden mock-up of the front fuselage of a two-seat Hunter in the experimental shop at Kingston. (*RAF Museum*)

Hunter T.7 prototype XJ615 with the original canopy fairing, which caused aerodynamic problems. (*BAE Systems*)

Bill Bedford (left-hand seat) and Hugh Mereweather (right-hand seat) in Hunter prototype XJ615. (*RAF Museum*)

Hunter T.7 prototype X615 at Dunsfold, fitted with experimental canopy fairing. (*BAE Systems*)

Hunter T.7 prototype XJ615, fitted with the production canopy fairing. (*BAE Systems*)

Hunter T.7 prototype XJ615 in a smart promotional colour scheme. (*RAF Museum*)

Early on in the flight test programme, while the systems were already well proven, there was severe local airflow instability around the fairing aft of the canopy. To overcome this problem, an extended aerodynamic flight development programme was initiated to establish the optimum shape. A variety of canopy and fairing shapes were tested, and by mid-1956 a design shaped to comply with the area rule was adopted. By this time the new variant had been designated the Hunter T.Mk 7, and production orders were placed for the RAF. Meanwhile, Hawker had been authorised to develop a trainer version based on the F.6, powered by the more powerful Avon Mk 203. A second prototype, XJ627, was completed to this configuration and made its first flight with the new hood fairing on 17 November 1956. While the T.7s had the gun pack removed, the second prototype was armed with two 30-mm cannons. In addition to new production, a number of the F.4s were returned to Hawker for conversion from single-seat to two-seat by simply changing the nose section. The T.7 also had a tail parachute fitted to reduce its landing run. Following its trials programme at Boscombe Down, XJ627 was delivered to Martin Baker airfield at Chalgrove on 19 November 1958 for ejection-seat development over a period of ten years. To protect the pilot from the blast of the departing seat, a metal shield was fitted between the seats and the plexiglass canopy on the starboard side was removed. The aircraft was used for many high-speed and low-level seat trials.

The plan had been initially to produce the trainers at Blackpool, but with the reduction in F.6 orders, the production of new T.7s was centred at Kingston.

Hunter T.7 XJ627, the second prototype, which appeared in the SBAC air display in September 1957. (*RAF Museum*)

XL563, the first of sixty-five aircraft, made its first flight on 11 October 1957. Ten of the production batch were exported to the Netherlands and another ten were allocated to the FAA as T.8s fitted with naval equipment. The main external change was the addition of an airfield arrester hook under the rear fuselage. The hook was not stressed for landings on aircraft carriers. The Netherlands placed an order for a further ten Hunter trainers direct with Hawker Aircraft, and these were delivered during 1958. N-320, the last of the ten T.7s bound for the Netherlands, was delivered in January 1959. It became PH-NLH with the NLR (the Royal Netherlands Aerospace Centre) as a trials aircraft. A number of modifications were made, including a fin-tip trailing aerial, an electronic pod on the inboard port pylon, and a nose probe. Among other trials, the aircraft was used for high-altitude nuclear radiation sample gathering.

The prototype Hunter T.8 WW664 was converted from a damaged F.4 airframe and had its first flight on 3 March 1958. It was followed by the first production aircraft, XL580, which flew on 30 May the same year. With the new production batch completed, a further seventeen F.4s were converted. When TACAN (tactical air navigation system) equipment was introduced to the RAF for measuring distance and bearing to a surface beacon, there was a limited batch conversion in the two-seaters, redesignated T.7A. Likewise, when the FAA introduced TACAN in the mid-1960s, four further F.4s were converted to become the Mk 8B, and another eleven with partial TACAN were designated Mk 8Cs. In both conversions the Aden gun pack and radar-ranging system were removed.

No. 229 OCU at Chivenor used the T.7 more than any other RAF unit. The type was first delivered there in May 1958, and despite being powered by the F.4's less powerful Avon, the T.7 closely replicated the flying characteristics of the more powerful F.6. The T.7s operated alongside F.6s and later FGA.9s for both UK and overseas students. With the withdrawal of Hunters from front-line service, 229 OCU duties evolved into preparing pilots for the operation of Phantoms, Lightnings, Buccaneers and Jaguars. The Hunters were therefore filling the gap between advanced pilot training at 4 FTS Valley and the type OCUs.

No. 229 OCU operated as three shadow squadrons: No. 63, which formed on 1 June 1963; No. 79, which formed in January 1967; and No. 234, which formed in November 1958. They often carried the relevant markings. The responsibility for training 4 FTS graduate pilots was shared between 63 and 234 Squadrons. This included instrument flying, formation flying, tactical air combat, weapons firing with air-to-ground cannon and SNEB rockets, and dive-bombing, usually on the Pembrey range. This was followed by air-to-air gun firing and low-level navigation, and was completed with simulated attacks. The total course took around eighty flying hours. Air-to-air gunnery target banners were towed by Meteor F.8s, which were later replaced by 79 Squadron FGA.9s, also capable of towing banners. No. 79 Squadron was responsible for training new instructors for all front-line fast jets and refreshing pilots who had completed a ground tour, ready to return to flying.

Production Hunter T.7 XL571 was delivered on 22 July 1958 and served with IRS, 92 Squadron in Blue Diamonds colours, and 229 OCU at Chivenor. It was lost off Strumble Head on 8 September 1977. (*BAE Systems*)

Hunter T.7 XF310 at Dunsfold, converted from an F.4. (*RAF Museum*)

Hunter T.7 XL568 in original RAF training colours of overall silver with yellow bands. It visited Hatfield in July 1967 from RAE Bedford. (*Philip Birtles*)

Dutch Hunter T.7 PH-NLH at Greenham Common, June 1979. (*Philip Birtles*)

The prototype conversion of a Hunter F.4 into T.8 WW664 for the FAA, carrying underwing fuel tanks. (*RAF Museum*)

Hunter T.7 XL593 of 229 OCU on approach to Bassingbourn in April 1968. (*Philip Birtles*)

Hunter T.7 XL592 no. 93 of 145 Squadron, previously with 229 OCU. (*Newark Air Museum*)

Hunter T.7 XL569, marked 85/ES with 234 Squadron, with 229 OCU. (*Newark Air Museum*)

Hunter T.7 XL617 no. 95 of 229 OCU at Chivenor, August 1969. (*Philip Birtles*)

Hunter T.7 XL618 no. 87 of 229 OCU, in camouflage. (*Philip Birtles*)

Hunter T.7 XL593 no. 92 of 229 OCU at Wattisham, April 1968. (*Philip Birtles*)

Chivenor closed in 1974 and the Hunters moved to Brawdy, replacing FAA Hunters, where the TWU (tactical weapons unit) formed to fill the gap between advanced jet-flying training and the front-line tactical OCUs. This provided a preview to operating aircraft as weapons systems. A major limitation at Brawdy was poor weather, which delayed pilot training. When, after the retirement of the V-Force, a greater number of fast-jet pilots was required, a second TWU with a better weather record, access to gunnery ranges and low flying capability was needed. Lossiemouth was chosen as the base for 2 TWU with its thirty Hunter F.6s and T.7s. No. 1 TWU, meanwhile, remained at Brawdy. With the new Hawk T.1s being delivered from April 1981, 2 TWU moved back to Chivenor with its Hawks while the Hunters returned to Brawdy. The last of them was finally retired at the end of 1984.

In 1971, Hunters partly equipped 237 OCU, which formed at Honington. The T.7s and T.8s were fitted with the Buccaneer S.2 Integrated Flight Instrument System (IFIS), designed to assist aircrew training for 12 and 15 Squadrons. The OCU later moved to Lossiemouth where it was disbanded in 1991. The special IFIS Hunter T.7/8 remained with the Buccaneer force until 208 Squadron disbanded on 31 March 1994, bringing to a close the RAF service of both the Hunter and Buccaneer.

Despite the diminutive Folland Gnat being chosen as the advanced jet trainer, a number of Hunter T.7s and F.6s served with 4 FTS at Valley, particularly if the student pilot was too tall to fit into the Gnat cockpit. In addition to direct training requirements, many of the operational squadrons or station flights were

Hunter T.7 XL619 no. 06 of 2 TWU at Greenham Common, July 1979. (*RAF Museum*)

Line-up of TWU Hunters at Brawdy in August 1976, including T.7 XL595 no. 98. (*RAF Museum*)

Hunter T.7 XF967 of 237 OCU at Finningley, September 1992. It has an overall matt black finish, celebrating forty years of the Hawker Hunter. (*Philip Birtles*)

Hunter T.7 XL614 O of 237 OCU. (*Newark Air Museum*)

Hunter T.8 WV322 of 237 OCU was delivered as an F.4 on 28 June 1955 and served with 43 and 92 Squadrons. It returned to HAL in 1959 for conversion to a T.8 and was operated by 764 NAS and 237 OCU. It was used for ground training at Cranwell with 284 Training Squadron as 9096M and was sold in November 2000, flying to Kemble with Delta Jets as G-BZSE. It moved to Exeter in June 2004. (*Author's collection*)

No. 237 OCU Hunter T.7 XL613 airborne from Honington over the east coast of England. (*RAF Museum*)

Hunter T.7 XL573 of 12 Squadron in support of the Buccaneer fleet in 1990. (*Newark Air Museum*)

Hunter T.7B XF967 with 12 Squadron at Honington in May 1970. (*Philip Birtles*)

issued with one or two Hunter T.7s for continuation training, instrument tests and communications. Other units to use Hunter T.7s included the Fighter Combat School, the Instrument Rating Squadron and the CFE. Both the Black Arrows and Blue Diamonds operated Hunter T.7s in the full display liveries.

As a flight test observer could be carried in the right-hand seat, a number of Hunter T.7s were issued to the government establishments at Farnborough, Bedford and Boscombe Down to assist in weapons and systems development. Some aircraft were used in pure research such as the Institute of Aviation Medicine. Hunters, including T.7s, also operated with the ETPS (Empire Test Pilots' School) at Farnborough and later at Boscombe Down.

The ETPS at Farnborough began receiving single-seat Hunter F.1s on 21 September 1954, starting with WT621, but the short endurance limited the scope of training test exercises. In July 1959, Hunter F.1s were replaced with improved-endurance F.4s. The T.7 prototype XJ615 was also delivered. The T.7 allowed instructors to fly with the students and demonstrate transonic and supersonic characteristics. For many students it was the first time they had exceeded the speed of sound. Sadly XJ615 was lost in a fatal accident when it hit high ground near Haslemere in Surrey on 24 June 1964. The Hunter F.4s were replaced by more effective F.6s from January 1965, and XE587 and XF375 became long-term residents of the ETPS. The F.6s were retired from the ETPS by May 1982.

The airfield at Farnborough had become congested by 1967, with commercial development on the boundaries and increasingly restricted airspace overhead due to air traffic for Heathrow. In January 1968 a move was made to Boscombe Down, where the ETPS had been originally formed on 21 June 1943. One advantage of moving to Boscombe Down was that the A&AEE operated a fleet of current combat aircraft

Hunter T.7 XL567 no. 84 of 4 FTS at Leeming in November 1967, in old colours with dayglow patches on light grey. (*Philip Birtles*)

Hunter T.7 WV372 no. 85 of 4 FTS in new red-and-white livery, visiting Hatfield in October 1973. (*Philip Birtles*)

Hunter T.7 XL610 of the 111 Squadron 'Black Arrows' at Coltishall. (*Author's collection*)

Hunter T.7 XL609 of 56 Squadron at Coltishall. (*Author's collection*)

Hunter T.7 XL621 of 4 Squadron at Gutersloh in June 1969. (*J. Mounce*)

Hunter T.7 XF321 of both 43 and 8 Squadrons over Aden. (*BAE Systems*)

Hunter T.7 XL565 of both 8 and 43 Squadrons in Aden, with FGA.9 XF511 of 43 Squadron in 1967. (*RAF Museum*)

Hunter F.6 XF375 of 6 ETPS at Biggin Hill in September 1964. (*Philip Birtles*)

which allowed for better maintenance support for the one-off types kept by the ETPS. The previous air traffic restrictions were also overcome. Hunter T.7s began arriving in May 1960, namely WV253, XL564, XL579 and XL612, in addition to the prototype. WV253 was an F.4 converted to a T.7. It was delivered to the ETPS on 12 June 1962 for spinning experience but was lost off Lyme Regis on 15 July 1968. XL564 was the second production T.7, joining the ETPS after trials with the A&AEE. It crashed 10 miles from Boscombe on 6 August 1998 and was written off. XL579 was with the ETPS at Farnborough and moved to Boscombe Down. It was abandoned over Winterbourne Gunner on approach to Boscombe Down on 22 January 1976 and was written off. XL612 was delivered to the ETPS in 1968 and made its last flight on 10 August 2001. It was last seen semi-derelict at Swansea Airport in June 2017.

In addition to the ETPS, a number of mainly two-seat Hunters were operated at the establishments, including Farnborough, Bedford and Boscombe Down. The first production Hunter T.7, XL563, was delivered to Boscombe Down on 19 December 1957, and for two years, from January 1961, it was allocated the task of chase plane for the Bristol T.188, based at Filton. It was then issued to the Institute of Aviation Medicine based at Farnborough on 2 May 1963 until retirement in July 1993, when it was allocated maintenance serial 9218M with DRA on engineering training work until the school was closed in June 1994. It was then stripped of its internal equipment and made ready for external display outside the former No. 1 Officers' Mess, where it was finally placed on a plinth on 27 February 1995. Soon afterwards the RAF officers' mess became derelict, and on 25 March 1999 the Hunter was taken down to make way for the new

Hunter T.7 WV253 of 24 ETPS. (*Newark Air Museum*)

Hunter T.7 WV253 of the ETPS, with a nose probe. (*RAF Museum*)

ETPS Hunter T.7 WV383 at Abingdon Air Show. (*RAF Museum*)

Hunter T.7 XL564 of the ETPS at Boscombe Down, June 1992. (*Philip Birtles*)

Hunter T.7 XL579 of the ETPS visiting Hatfield in March 1970. (*Philip Birtles*)

Hunter T.7 XL612 of the ETPS at Fairford in July 1995. (*Philip Birtles*)

Hunter T.7 XL616 of the A&AEE Boscombe Down, March 1971. (*Philip Birtles*)

Aviator Hotel. The aircraft was stored at Kempston with the possibility of a return to flight. In March 2014 it was moved to Farnborough and then on to the FAST site in December, where it has been restored and is on display.

XF321 was another Farnborough-based Hunter T.7 with the RAE. After service with 130 Squadron as an F.4, it was converted in 1958 to a T.7 by HAL and served with 43 and 8 Squadrons in the Middle East, and then in 1417 Flight. It joined RAE Farnborough in 1976 and was written off in a wheels-up landing at Bedford on 28 May 1984. Following this it was used for ground instruction as A2734 at Manadon. In addition to serving with the ETPS, Hunter T.7 XL612 also served with Aero Flight at RAE Bedford, where it was recorded in November 1971. Also recorded at Boscombe Down in March 1971 was T.7A XL616, which was originally delivered to 19 MU on 3 February 1959. It operated with 19 Squadron in 1966. With the temporary grounding of the Buccaneer fleet, XL616 was used as a continuation trainer at Laarbruch. It served with 1 TWU at Brawdy in 1985, and when retired, it was allocated 9223M. See Chapter 9.

Supporting the introduction of the Harrier was T.7 XL596, which carried the markings of 4 Squadron at Wittering in June 1970. On the same flight line was T.7 XL601 with Wittering Station Flight. Both were with the Harrier Conversion Unit, which later became 233 OCU. XL596 crashed at Shawbury on 2 November 1973, killing both pilots. XL601 had also served with West Raynham Station Flight in 1968, while the Hunter FGA.9s of 1 and 54 Squadrons were based there, and later with Wittering Station Flight.

Hunter T.8s were used on second-line duties with the FAA, initially with 700Z Flight from 1961 until the following year. WW664 was the first to convert to the

Hunter T.7 XL563 of the Institute of Aviation Medicine at Boscombe Down in June 1992. (*Philip Birtles*)

Hunter T.7 XF321 of RAE Farnborough at Leuchars in September 1981. (*Philip Birtles*)

Hunter T.7 XL612 of Aero Flight RAE Bedford in November 1971. (*Philip Birtles*)

Hunter T.7 XL596 of 4 Squadron at Wittering, June 1970. (*Philip Birtles*)

Hunter T.7 XL601 of Wittering Station Flight, June 1970. (*Philip Birtles*)

T.8 in 1957. When 700B Flight formed to bring the Buccaneer S.2 into FAA service, a pair of Hunter T.8s were used for pilot familiarisation. No. 738 NAS was the Jet Conversion NAFS (Naval Air Fighter School), which operated Hunter T.8s from June 1962 until it disbanded in May 1970. No. 759 NAS reformed at Brawdy on 1 August 1963 as the Naval Advanced Flying Training School, equipped with Hunter T.8s and T.8Cs until it was disbanded in December 1969. From 1958, 764 NAS flew Hunter T.8s and later T.8Cs from Lossiemouth for air warfare instructor training until it was disbanded in July 1972. No. 800B Flight, which was formed for service trials with the Scimitar, also used at least one Hunter T.8B. When undertaking the conversion of pilots to Sea Harrier FRS.1s, in addition to two-seat Harrier T.4Ns, three Hunters were converted to T.8Ms, standard-fitted with Blue Fox radar in the nose for airborne training with the system.

Airwork Services' civilian-operated Fleet Requirements and Air Director Unit (FRADU) moved from Hurn to RNAS Yeovilton (HMS *Heron*) in 1972, and Hunter T.8s were among the types operated. Many were fitted with Harley lights in the nose to assist with visual tracking. Also at Yeovilton was the busy station flight, known as 'Heron' Flight, which operated a number of T.8s on a variety of duties, including instrument and continuation training, as well as the Naval Flying Standards Flight. In addition, Heron Flight was responsible for three Flag Officer Naval Air Command (FONAC) special-painted 'Admiral's Barge' Hunter T.8s, reserved for flying senior officers on official duties.

Mk 12 XE531, converted from a Mk 6 and powered by an Avon 203, was a unique two-seat Hunter. It was ordered by the RAE to evaluate the planned TSR-2 strike-bomber radar. The aircraft was delivered to Farnborough on 8 February 1963, and following the cancellation of the TSR-2, it remained at Farnborough and Bedford on systems development work, which included a trial installation of a large vertical survey camera mounted in the nose. It was also fitted with a head-up display (HUD). Its advanced instrumentation fit was of great benefit to Harrier development. XE531 was written off in a crash after take-off on 17 March 1982.

Hunter T.8 XL598, marked 778/BY, of 738 NAS at Odiham, September 1968. (*Philip Birtles*)

Hunter T.8 XF995, marked 698/LM, of 764 NAS at Hatfield, October 1967. (*Philip Birtles*)

Hunter T.8 WV322, marked 239/LM, of 809 NAS at Hatfield, June 1965. (*Philip Birtles*)

Hunter T.8M XL602 with Blue Fox radar in the nose. (*BAE Systems*)

Hunter T.8M XL602. (*BAE Systems*)

Hunter T.8M XL580 of 899 NAS with a Sea Harrier and Harrier T.4N. (*BAE Systems*)

Hunter T.8 WT772, marked 736/VL, of FRU at Hatfield, July 1972. (*Philip Birtles*)

Hunter T.8 WT702, marked 747/VL, of the FRADU at Hatfield, July 1973. (*Philip Birtles*)

The first production Hunter T.8, XL580, in service with Airwork-operated FRADU at Yeovilton in August 1970. (*Philip Birtles*)

Hunter T.8 XL584 of 744 FRU, fitted with a Harley light, at Yeovilton in July 1972. (*Philip Birtles*)

Hunter T.8 XL582 of Yeovilton Station Flight, September 1967. (*Philip Birtles*)

Hunter T.8 XF321, marked 728/VL, of Naval Flying Standards Flight/Heron Flight at Yeovilton in July 1972. The same serial number was also carried by a T.7—see page 158, bottom. (*Philip Birtles*)

Hunter T.8 XL584, marked 18/VL, of FONFT at Yeovilton, September 1969. (*Philip Birtles*)

The sole Hunter T.12, XE531, with RAE Farnborough at Greenham Common, July 1976. (*Philip Birtles*)

6

The Tactical Hunters

The Hunter FGA.9s were all conversions of earlier F.6s, optimised for fighter ground attack to provide a close-support capability for RAF 38 Group in Strike Command during the 1960s. The aircraft was originally optimised for service in hot climates like the Middle East, where many of the airfields were spartan, requiring the installation of a rear-fuselage-mounted tail-braking chute and improved cooling for the cockpit. With the government policy of withdrawing gradually from the Middle East and Asia and reducing the RAF presence, there was a need to be ready to deploy to distant countries at short notice. As a result, the 230-gallon fuel drop tank became a standard fit. It was also a requirement for the drop tank installation to be stressed for ground-attack operations, with a strut being fitted between the non-jettisonable tank and the wing, in addition to mounting on the pylon. Because of the greater endurance offered, pilot oxygen supply was increased.

With the retirement of the ground-attack Venoms in RAF Germany in 1958, the AFDS at the CFE started an evaluation of the requirement for the most suitable replacement, using the Jet Provost and the Gnat. Although the Hunter was considered too expensive for the role, Hawker modified a pair of F.6s—XK150 and XK151—with tail chutes to participate in the trials. Following these highly successful trials, Hawker was instructed to produce a Hunter optimised for the ground-attack role.

Modifications were incorporated with production F.6s already completed, and an initial order for forty FGA.9s was placed in 1958, with Hawker and RAF working parties completing the reconfigurations at Horsham St Faith for thirty-six interim aircraft still powered by the Avon 203. These were later brought up to full modification with the Avon 207. In addition to improved cockpit ventilation and an overload fuel tank, a small section of the flaps was removed to give clearance for the larger fuel tank, while a tail parachute, similar to that fitted to the T.7, was introduced for shorter landings in hot climates and high altitudes. The gun-blast deflectors were omitted as they were considered unnecessary for the low-level role. The four underwing pylons were configured to carry 100- or 230-gallon fuel tanks, or 100-gallon fuel tanks loaded with napalm could be carried on any position.

With the FGA.9's strengthened wings, each inboard pylon could carry 1,000-lb or 500-lb bombs and six 3-inch rocket projectiles (RP) or a battery of either twenty-four or thirty-seven 2-inch folding-fin unguided rockets. For practice, a carrier holding a pair of 25-lb bombs could be used. Individual positions were capable of carrying four Mk 12 rocket rails, each carrying up to four RP with 60-lb explosive heads. All this was in addition to the standard four Aden 30-mm cannons, providing a greater destructive capability. The resulting aircraft was robust, manoeuvrable and versatile, but it could have been considerably better if the government had invested more funds into its development. Internal fuel capacity was not increased.

The Hunter FR.10 was an additional production F.6 modification programme. The prototype, XF429, was first flown on 7 November 1959. The FR.10 retained the cannon armament of the F.6 and the radar ranging system in the nose, along with a pack installed with oblique cameras on either side of the nose. A contract was issued by the MOS (Ministry of Supply) in 1959 for thirty-two aircraft. Five were completed by 28 November 1960, when the first example was delivered to 19 MU at St Athan.

While most Fighter Command squadrons re-equipped with Lightnings, a small number also took FGA.9s on charge, and in the Middle East they were to see action. With the Kuwait crisis of 1961, when Iraq laid claim to the territory, Hunter FGA.9 squadrons based at Khormaksar in Aden and Eastleigh in Nairobi were rapidly deployed to Muharraq in Bahrain, ready to move into Kuwait. In the event, however, the Hunters were not called into combat. When the situation became unstable in

Hunter FGA.9 prototype conversion XG135 at 5 MU Kemble. (*BAE Systems*)

Hunter FGA.9 XE592 production conversion at Dunsfold. (*RAF Museum*)

Hunter FGA.9 showing the range of weapons and underwing stores capable of being carried by this version. The only weapons not carried operationally were Fireflash and Firestreak under the Hunter wingtips. This photograph was staged at Dunsfold in 1958. (*BAE Systems*)

Hunter FGA.9 XG252 at 60 MU Leconfield in July 1970. (*Philip Birtles*)

Hunter FGA.9 XG260 T of 229 OCU at Chivenor in August 1969. (*Philip Birtles*)

Hunter 100-gallon underwing fuel drop tanks. (*Newark Air Museum*)

Hunter FR.10 prototype XF429 at Dunsfold with underwing fuel drop tanks. (*RAF Museum*)

Hunter FR.10 XE621 in production conversion at Dunsfold. (*RAF Museum*)

Aden in the early 1960s, Hunters were called into action to defend against local tribal terrorists. The rules of engagement required all strikes to be preceded by leaflet drops to give warning to local civilians that an attack was planned. This generally resulted in the terrorists taking cover in surrounding hills and making a return to the village after the attack. An example of a more concentrated ground attack by Aden Hunters is as follows: It would start with a FGA.9 and FR.10 taking off for the target fifteen minutes ahead of the attack; the FGA.9, with leaflets in the flaps, would release the leaflets over the target while the FR.10 took photographs as evidence of the warning; the main force of between four and eight FGA.9s would then attack using the 30-mm cannons and rockets, with the leaflet-carrying aircraft flying top cover; when the attack was complete, the FR.10 would make a final pass to record the damage.

The RAF FGA.9 squadrons employed in actions in the Middle East were numbers 8, 43 and 208. In May 1960, 43 Squadron began to replace its Hunter F.6s with FGA.9s at Leuchars, and on 21 June 1961 a move was made to Nicosia in Cyprus, where the squadron stayed until relocating to Khormaksar in Aden on 1 March 1963. It remained operating from Aden until it was disbanded on 7 November 1967. No. 8 Squadron had spent all of its post-First World War service life in the Middle East, reforming at Helwan in Egypt on 18 October 1920. The squadron converted from Meteor FR.9s to fourteen Hunter FGA.9s at Khormaksar in January 1960, adding four Hunter FR.10s in April 1961 until May 1963. There were also two T.7s on charge. The squadron moved around the Middle East during 1961, including to Bahrain, before returning to Aden. It relocated to Muharraq in September 1967, when FR.10s rejoined the unit, and was disbanded on 21 December 1967. No. 208 Squadron was another unit based in the Middle East for a long time. Following service in France during the First World War, it reformed at Ismailia on 1 February 1920. The squadron flew Hunter F.6s from Nicosia from March 1958 and disbanded on 31 March 1959. In March 1960, 208 Squadron reformed at Stradishall and moved to Eastleigh on 3 June, before going to the

Middle East in June 1961 and then ending up at Khormaksar with twelve FGA.9s and one T.7 in November of the same year. In June 1964 the squadron moved to Muharraq, where it disbanded on 10 September 1971. During operations by 8 and 208 Squadrons in the Middle East, a total of 527 missions were flown, with some 176,000 rounds of 30-mm ammunition fired in addition to 2,500 RP. The combined role of 8 and 208 Squadrons was to support British and Arab army units policing not just the Aden Protectorate, but the entire Middle East Command area from Kenya, 1,000 miles to the south, to Bahrain, some 1,300 miles to the north.

There were periods when operations were relatively calm, with training and familiarisation of new pilots in the area being the main activity, and times also of intensive active combat. In July 1961 General Kassim of Iraq brought his forces to the borders of Kuwait in preparation for an invasion to capture the oil fields. No. 8 Squadron was rapidly deployed to Kuwait to defend against the Iraqi forces, and 208 Squadron, then based at Eastleigh in Kenya, was ordered to Bahrain as support for 8 Squadron. Meanwhile, 43 Squadron was moved from Leuchars to Cyprus. In addition, forces were rapidly increased in the Gulf region with deployments from Europe and other Middle Eastern bases. These movements left General Kassim in no doubt that the British intended to defend Kuwait, and thus he withdrew.

There was concern that a total withdrawal of British forces from the Gulf would prompt Iraq to act aggressively towards Kuwait. The decision was made, therefore, to maintain a Hunter squadron in Bahrain by basing 8 and 208 Squadrons from Khormaksar on a two-month rotation. In Aden, following repeated strafing attacks on villages close to the border by Yemeni Air Force Mig-15s, the Hunter squadrons

Hunter FGA.9 XK151 X of 8 Squadron with its air brake deployed over Aden. (*Author's collection*)

Hunter FGA.9 XE532 K of 208 Squadron in the Middle East. (*Author's collection*)

Hunter FGA.9 taking off from Belhan strip in Aden. (*RAF Museum*)

Hunter FGA.9 XJ692 T of 43 and 208 Squadrons over Aden. (*Author's collection*)

MEAF Hunter FGA.9 XG256 H armed with underwing RP. (*Author's collection*)

Hunter FGA.9 XG237 T of 8 Squadron, Aden. (*BAE Systems*)

Hunter FGA.9 XG152 of 208 Squadron, Aden. (*BAE Systems*)

began to operate dawn-to-dusk patrols as a deterrent. Pilots and ground crew were split into shifts, one from 06.00 to 13.00 hrs and the other from 12.00 to 19.00 hrs. At the start, two Hunters would take-off at dawn and fly north-east up the coast to Yemen, and then turn west to fly along the indistinct mountainous border before returning to base. Additional pairs would take off at hourly intervals, with all aircraft being fully armed and carrying long-range underwing fuel tanks, allowing an endurance of around one and a half hours. In addition, Hunters were maintained at readiness in support of army units up country. Air and ground crews were challenged by the high utilisation of the aircraft, and aircraft serviceability became critical. Relief was provided by a detachment of eight 1 Squadron FGA.9s from October 1962, but after one month the detachment returned to the UK. In January 1963 there was a 54 Squadron detachment to Aden for a month to provide some relief for 208 Squadron, but in March, 43 Squadron moved from Cyprus to become part of the Khormaksar Tactical Wing. As well as the three Hunter squadrons, there were 37 Squadron Shackletons and 26 Squadron Belvederes. The four Hunter FR.10s and both T.7s from 8 Squadron, as well as a T.7 from each of 43 and 208 Squadrons, were reallocated to a reformed 1417 Flight, with five photo-reconnaissance pilots and fifteen ground crew. This gave a formidable force of forty-six Hunters, which were in regular action up to the final withdrawal in 1967.

In the UK, 38 Group reformed on 1 January 1960 as part of RAF Air Support Command, similar to the modern-day Tactical Expeditionary Force. It consisted of Hunter FGA.9s with 1 and 54 Squadrons at Stradishall, while Javelins of 64 Squadron at Waterbeach provided all-weather defence. The group also included logistical support from transport aircraft—the Beverley, the Hastings and the Pioneer—together with helicopter support from the Sycamore, the Belvedere and the Whirlwind. No. 1 Squadron re-equipped from Hunter F.6s to FGA.9s in January 1960, moving to Waterbeach in November 1961, West Raynham in August 1963, and Wittering in July 1969, when it re-equipped with Harriers. No. 54 Squadron similarly replaced its Hunter F.6s with FGA.9s in March 1960, moving with 1 Squadron to Waterbeach and West Raynham until going to Coningsby in September 1969 to re-equip with Phantom FGR.2s. The Hunter FGA.9s with 38 Group provided an effective close-support capability until the Harrier entered service.

No. 45 Squadron reformed at West Raynham with FGA.9s on 1 August 1972, and moved to Wittering in September 1972. While at Wittering the squadron was joined by 58 Squadron, which had reformed from a nucleus of 45 Squadron pilots on 1 August 1973. The duty of both squadrons was in the ground-attack role, and to maintain experience for newly qualified students who were to join the Jaguar force while sufficient numbers of the type were delivered to the RAF. The Hunters also provided an additional ground-attack capability. Both squadrons were disbanded on 26 July 1976. Also at Wittering were a small number of Hunter T.7s and FGA.9s with the Harrier Conversion Team, which later became 233 OCU.

The three reserve squadrons with 229 OCU at Chivenor not only had instructional duties, but were an operational reserve as low-level air defence of Britain. They would exercise two or three times a year from the east coast

Hunter FR.10 XE599 of 1417 Flight, Aden. (*RAF Museum*)

Hunter FGA.9 XE616 P of 1 Squadron at West Raynham, September 1968. (*Philip Birtles*)

Hunter FGA.9 XG130 of 1 Squadron after a landing mishap at El Adem, 1 May 1969. (*RAF Museum*)

Hunter FGA.9 XG264 D of 54 Squadron at West Raynham in September 1968. (*Philip Birtles*)

Hunter FGA.9 XE582 no. 70 of 45 Squadron at Biggin Hill, September 1975. (*Philip Birtles*)

Hunter FGA.9 XJ686 no. 41 of 58 Squadron at Greenham Common, July 1976. (*Philip Birtles*)

Hunter FGA.9 XF430 N of the Harrier Conversion Unit at Wittering in June 1970. (*Philip Birtles*)

front-line bases at Wattisham, Coningsby, Binbrook and Leuchars, from where they would fly combat air patrols (CAPs). Permanent Hunter FGA.9 detachments of 79 Squadron were also maintained at Gibraltar to protect RAF aircraft operating from the base. When not allocated to specific tasks, or on standby, daily reconnaissance sorties were flown over anchored Russian ships off the North African coast. Three TWU pilots manned the detachment, with pilots rotated every week. The detachment was finally withdrawn on 3 August 1978 after around twelve years of service.

Although the Hunter FGA.9 was planned to replace Venom ground-attack aircraft in RAF Germany, none of the squadrons based there were to operate the new version. However, further afield in Asia, 20 Squadron was reformed at Tengah in Singapore on 1 September 1961 to serve in the Malayan Emergency, also known as the Anti-British National Liberation War. This was followed, in May 1962, by 28 Squadron re-equipping with FGA.9s at Kai Tak in Hong Kong. The Hunters were withdrawn upon the disbandment of the squadron on 2 January 1967. A total of 128 Hunter F.6s were converted to FGA.9s, including the interim batch of F.6As. In addition to thirty-six interim aircraft at Horsham St Faith, nine were converted at 5 MU Kemble and the remainder by the company, which by then was part of Hawker Siddeley Aviation (HSA).

The FR.10 served with 2 and IV Squadrons in RAF Germany more than with any other squadrons. No. IV Squadron introduced the version at Gutersloh in December 1960, together with the Swift FR.5. The Swifts were withdrawn in March 1961 when the squadron moved to Jever. On 6 September 1961 the squadron returned to Gutersloh where it was disbanded on 30 May 1970. In March 1961 the Swifts of 2 Squadron at Gutersloh were replaced by FR.10s. The squadron was disbanded at Gutersloh on 31 March 1971. Most of these

Hunter FGA.9 XF419 D of 79 Squadron at Chivenor in August 1969. (*Philip Birtles*)

Hunter FGA.9 XG194 A of 79 Squadron at Coltishall in September 1974 with toned-down RAF markings. (*Philip Birtles*)

Hunter FGA.9 XG196 no. 25 of 234 Squadron/TWU at Greenham Common, July 1976. (*Philip Birtles*)

Hunter FGA.9 XJ687 O of 79 Squadron on standby at Gibraltar, April 1976. (*Philip Birtles*)

Hunter FGA.9 XK141 no. 33 of 1 TWU at Brawdy, July 1980. (*Philip Birtles*)

Hunter FGA.9 XE624 G of 1 TWU at Leuchars in September 1981 with the 12 Squadron zap below the cockpit. (*Philip Birtles*)

Hunter FGA.9 XF445 Q of 2 TWU at Greenham Common, June 1979. (*Philip Birtles*)

No. 2 Squadron Hunter FR.10s XE621 H, XF432 S and XJ639 C in formation with a Swift FR.5, also of 2 Squadron, over Germany. (*Newark Air Museum*)

squadron aircraft were bought by Hawker Siddeley and delivered to Dunsfold for refurbishment and sale overseas. A number of other squadrons, including No. 8 at Khormaksar, also operated a small number of FR.10s for reconnaissance support for local ground forces.

The two RAF Germany FR.10 squadrons were allocated to NATO as the principal tactical reconnaissance force based at Gutersloh under the control of the Tactical Operation Centre, flying over an area from the Mediterranean to Norway. Each squadron had its own support team of army ground liaison officers who worked with a mobile field photographic unit, which processed the film after each sortie. The photos were then analysed and the results passed on to the NATO chain of command. The Hunter FR.10 pilots with 2 and IV Squadrons soon became accepted as the premier low-level high-speed visual reconnaissance asset. In the annual 'Royal Flush' exercises, the two squadrons regularly beat the American, French and German participants thanks to the high flexibility and superior manoeuvrability of the Hunter under operational conditions.

In Yemen, 1417 Flight was part of the Khormaksar Strike Wing when the crisis escalated in 1964. Three Hunter FR.10s replaced Meteor FR.9s in time to take part in the Radfan operations. With the poor mapping of the area, the FR.10s were able to illuminate targets, reducing the time taken to track the rebels. The Radfan activities had reduced by mid-June 1964, after which the flight's FR.10s had flown close to 120 sorties with thousands of images taken, and had fired nearly 8,000 rounds from their Aden cannons.

Hunter FR.4 WT780 was used to develop the role of the later FR.10 with a camera installation in the nose. (*RAF Museum*)

Hunter FR.10 XF432 S of 2 Squadron. (*Newark Air Museum*)

Hunter FR.10 XJ633 S of 2 Squadron at Dunsfold in August 1971 with camera nose installation. (*Philip Birtles*)

Hunter FR.10 XE585 E of 2 Squadron at Dunsfold in August 1971 after retirement from the RAF. It was converted to a T.66S for the Indian Air Force and delivered on 13 December 1973. (*Philip Birtles*)

Hunter FR.10 XF438 E of 4 Squadron at Dunsfold in June 1970 after retirement from the RAF. It was converted to a Swiss F.58A as J-4102 and delivered on 24 December 1971. (*Philip Birtles*)

Hunter FR.10 XE596 no. 13 of 220 OCU with a white spine at Chivenor, August 1969. (*Philip Birtles*)

Hunter FR.10 XF426 no. 12 of 229 OCU. (*Author's collection*)

Just as the Hunter was finally being retired from RAF use, the Buccaneer fleet was grounded due to wing fatigue problems. These problems caused two fatal accidents, the second being with XV Squadron on 7 February 1980 during a Red Flag exercise at Nellis in the USA. On inspection of the Buccaneer fleet it was found the outer wings suffered from fatigue, and while some were repairable, others were not. Those that could be repaired were going to be out of service for some time. For the pilots to maintain flying practice, a number of Hunter T.7s, F.6As and FGA.9s were taken out of storage and brought back into service with 12, 15 and 16 Squadrons. In addition, 216 Squadron, which was in the process of forming, also received a small batch of Hunters. With a reduced number of Buccaneers (due to some being deemed irreparable), 216 Squadron was absorbed into 12 Squadron in August 1980. When the Buccaneers were returned to service, beginning in August 1980, the stop-gap Hunters were returned to storage. F.6 XF383 was the last single-seat Hunter in RAF service when it was finally withdrawn from 12 Squadron at Lossiemouth in 1984.

The two later Hunter marks with the RAF in the UK, Middle East and Asia were highly effective in the tactical support of ground troops and logistics. This record helped to promote considerable export sales of many refurbished ex-RAF aircraft, and formed the basis for licensed production overseas. The aircraft was robust and well liked by the pilots once all the earlier problems had been overcome.

7

Navy Single-Seat Hunters

Following orders for Hunter T.8s by the Admiralty, further orders were placed for single-seat GA.11s, all of which were conversions of ex-RAF F.4s powered by Avon RA 120 turbojets. In most conversions the armament was removed and the aircraft was used for training with the Airwork-operated Fleet Requirements Unit (FRU) and the Air Director School (ADS), both based at Yeovilton. These were later amalgamated into the Fleet Requirements Air Direction Unit (FRADU). Naval radios and TACAN navigation systems were fitted with an airfield arrester hook under the rear fuselage. The early batch of F.4s selected were fitted with the pre-modification 228 wing which could only carry inboard pylons, while later, sixteen examples had stronger wings allowing all four underwing pylons to be attached, which could carry practice bombs or RP rails for weapons training. Some examples, designated PR.11s, were fitted with reconnaissance cameras by Short Brothers at Belfast, while others had Harley lights fitted in the nose for visual tracking when being used as targets. Trials were undertaken to carry either Sidewinder or Bullpup air-to-air missiles, but they were not adopted.

Conversions of low-hour F.4s started at Kingston with XE712 as the first GA.11. The aircraft was delivered to the A&AEE on 6 April 1962. The GA.11s were painted in gloss dark sea grey on the upper surfaces, and gloss white below, while a few also had a white dorsal spine. A total of forty F.4s were converted to the GA.11 configuration, with the first being delivered to 738 NAS at Lossiemouth in June 1962. Twelve GA.11s and six T.8s had been delivered by the end of the year.

No. 738 NAS was designated the Advanced Training Squadron and provided training in low-level navigation, ground attack and air-to-air weapons delivery. The Admiralty had hoped to increase the Hunter GA.11 strength substantially with the FAA, but funds were not available. This resulted in a small number of unmodified ex-RAF F.4s being transferred for a short period. With Lossiemouth becoming congested, 738 NAS moved to Brawdy on 1 January 1964, giving training in fighter tactics and weapons release to pupils from 759 NAS, which had become the Naval Advanced Flying Training School, equipped with T.8s. In 1967 an aerobatic team of four GA.11s was formed by 738 NAS. It was named

Hunter GA.11 WV380, a prototype converted from an F.4. (*RAF Museum*)

Hunter GA.11 WV380 on a pre-delivery test flight. It was originally delivered to the CAW at Manby on 11 August 1955 as an F.4. It returned to HAL in 1960 for conversion to a GA.11 and was delivered to 738 NAS at Lossiemouth on 29 May 1962. It went back to HSA on 24 April 1970 and was converted to an F.58A for Switzerland as J-4119. It was delivered on 3 November 1972. (*BAE Systems*)

Hunter PR.11 WT723 of 736 FRU at Yeovilton, September 1973. This aircraft was originally delivered as an F.4 to 5 MU on 25 March 1955. It served with 54 and 14 Squadrons before going to 229 OCU. It was converted to a GA.11 and delivered to 764 NAS in August 1962 and redesignated PR.11. It joined FRADU at Yeovilton until it was retired on 23 May 1993. It was allocated to Culdrose as A2616 for the SAH. By September 1997 it had been acquired by Classic Jet Aircraft at Exeter and was registered G-PR11 on 21 August 1999 as the oldest airworthy Hunter. (*Philip Birtles*)

Hunter GA.11 WT804, marked 831/VL, of the ADS at Greenham Common, June 1979. This aircraft was delivered in April 1955 to 247 Squadron as an F.4. After conversion to a GA.11, it was delivered to 738 NAS at Brawdy and was transferred to the FRU at Hurn. It moved to FRADU at Yeovilton in October 1972 and was retired to Shawbury in 1985. It was then allocated to the SAH at Culdrose as A2732 and then moved to the Fire Service College at Moreton-in-Marsh as A2646. (*Philip Birtles*)

Hunter PR.11 WT721, marked 694/LM, of 764 NAS with white spine at Lossiemouth in July 1970. This aircraft was delivered to 33 MU at Lyneham on 15 February 1955 as an F.4 and served with 54 Squadron. Following conversion to a GA.11, it was delivered to the A&AEE at Boscombe Down in December 1962. It was converted to a PR.11 at Lossiemouth and was destroyed in a crash near Blair Atholl on 22 September 1970. (*Philip Birtles*)

Hunter GA.11 WV382, marked 830/VL, of the FRU, fitted with a Harley light, at Yeovilton in September 1973. It is now preserved at the East Midlands Aeropark. This aircraft was delivered as an F.4 on 15 August 1955 and served with 67 and 112 Squadrons. It was then converted to a GA.11 by HAL and delivered to 738 NAS in August 1962, initially at Lossiemouth and then Brawdy. It joined the FRU at Hurn in April 1969 and moved to Yeovilton in October 1972. It was stored at Kemble and Shawbury before being allocated to ground training at Lee-on-Solent as A2730 in February 1985. It was then bought by the group at Long Marston, and was finally conserved at the East Midlands Aeropark. See Appendix I 'Survivors'. (*Philip Birtles*)

Hunter GA.11 XE674, marked 788/BY, of 738 NAS at Yeovilton, June 1969. This aircraft was delivered to 5 MU on 1 July 1955 as an F.4 and served with 112 and 234 Squadrons before conversion to a GA.11. It was issued to 738 NAS in June 1962 and bought back by HAL in April 1970, when it was converted into F.58A J-4124 and delivered to Switzerland on 19 January 1973. (*Philip Birtles*)

No. 738 NAS aerobatic team, the 'Rough Diamonds', displaying in GA.11s at Yeovilton in September 1968. (*Philip Birtles*)

Hunter GA.11 XF291, marked 789/BY, of 738 NAS 'Rough Diamonds' at Yeovilton in September 1969. This aircraft was delivered as an F.4 to 5 MU on 29 November 1955 and served with 67 and 112 Squadrons, returning to Kemble in May 1957 for conversion to a GA.11. It was then delivered to 738 NAS in June 1963, and in August 1964 returned to HAL for conversion to F.58A J-4118. It was assembled in Emmen. (*Philip Birtles*)

the 'Rough Diamonds' and led by Lieutenant Commander Chris Cummings. The team disbanded in 1969 and the squadron disbanded on 8 May 1970.

From July 1962 some Hunter T.8s with 764 NAS at Lossiemouth were replaced by GA.11s and PR.11s. The main task of these aircraft was air warfare instructor training. When it disbanded on 27 July 1972, 764 NAS had ten GA.11s and four T.8Cs.

The FRU based at Hurn began to re-equip with Hunter GA.11s in 1969, with the first two replacing Scimitars in March. Upon moving to Yeovilton, the unit became the FRADU. Among its duties was the simulation of sea-skimming anti-ship missiles to test ship defences, plus radio and radar calibration and gunnery tracking. By 1984 the unit strength was fourteen GA.11s and eight T.8s. The Hunters also flew practice interception sorties to train the ADS fighter controllers. In July 1975, FRADU formed a four-Hunter GA.11 aerobatic team named the 'Blue Herons'. It was unique in being the world's first jet aerobatic team with military jets flown by civilian pilots, although most of them came from a military background. The Blue Herons disbanded in 1980 due to budget cuts. At the end of 1983, Flight Refuelling took over the contract from Airwork, and by May 1995 the Hunter GA.11s had been replaced by Hawk T.1s.

Hunter GA.11 XF977, marked 695/LM, of 764 NAS in the circuit at Lossiemouth. This aircraft was delivered to 33 MU on 17 May 1956 as an F.4 and was operated by 118 Squadron from July 1956. It returned to HSA in 1962 for conversion to a GA.11 and was delivered to 738 NAS at Lossiemouth in October 1962. It moved to 764 NAS and was converted to a PR.11, fitted with F.95 cameras, before returning to 764 NAS. It was allocated to ADS at Yeovilton, which became FRADU, and was destroyed in a crash in the English Channel on 17 March 1981. (*Author's collection*)

Hunter PR.11 WT723, marked 692/LM, of 764 NAS at Hatfield in June 1968, with a white spine. See also top photograph on p. 186. (*Philip Birtles*)

Hunter GA.11 WW654 of 833 FRADU at Greenham Common in July 1976. Note the 'Blue Herons' logo on its underwing fuel tank. This aircraft was originally delivered to 5 MU on 28 March 1955 and served with 4 and 98 Squadrons, followed by 229 OCU. It was returned to HSA in 1961 for conversion to a GA.11 and served with 738 NAS at Lossiemouth from September 1962 until 1970, when it was stored. It was then issued to FRADU at Yeovilton until late 1986, when it was allocated to the SAH at Culdrose as A2754. It was retired in March 1993 and was moved to Portsmouth by December 1993. It is now displayed at the former RNAS Ford. See Appendix I. (*Philip Birtles*)

Hunter GA.11 XE685, marked 708/VL, of Yeovilton Station Flight at Hatfield, July 1969. This aircraft was originally delivered to 33 MU on 18 July 1955 as an F.4 and served with 98 and 93 Squadrons. It returned to HSA in 1960 for conversion to a GA.11 and was delivered to 764 NAS at Lossiemouth in May 1963. After storage at 5 MU it joined Yeovilton Station Flight in 1967 and then went to 764 NAS until 1972. It joined ADS in 1973 and then FRADU before being retired in 1994. It was sold as G-GAII with the Hunter Flying Club at Exeter. See Chapter 9. (*Philip Birtles*)

8

Hunter Exports

The Hunter was a great success in new export sales, production under license overseas and in the refurbishment of retired RAF and European aircraft. The first order came from Sweden, while Hunter F.4s were still being produced for the RAF. On 29 June 1954 the Swedish government placed an order for 120 Avon-powered single-seat fighters with the designation Mk 50, although in Swedish service it was known as J-34. The initial aircraft were powered by Avon 115s, which progressively improved to the surge-free Avon 119 and 120 standard. The first twenty-four aircraft were built at Kingston, with the remainder at Blackpool. The first of these aircraft, 34001, flew on 24 June 1955, and deliveries started on 26 August 1955 through to 1956. In Swedish service the Hunters equipped F8 Wing at Barkarby, F9 at Save, F10 at Angleholm and F18 at Tullinge, the latter forming an aerobatic team, the 'Aero-Hunters', in 1962. The Swedish Hunters retained the original wing planform with no leading edge dog-tooth extensions, and were armed with Sidewinder air-to-air missiles, increasing their potential considerably. In an effort to improve performance, a small number were fitted with a Flygmotor reheat system, but although it gave a substantial increase in thrust, speed was not increased greatly due to wing design. In the late 1960s, replacement of the Hunters started with deliveries of Saab Drakens, while the Hunters continued in the OTU task.

Only four days after the Swedish order was placed, Denmark signed a contract for thirty Hunters based on the F.4, numbered 401 to 430 and designated Mk 51, to replace their Meteor F.8s. The batch was built at Kingston, and the first flight of E-401 was on 15 December 1955. Deliveries were completed with E-430 arriving on 18 August 1956. Power came from Avon 115s, which were later modified to avoid engine surge when the guns were fired. The aircraft equipped Esk-724 at Aalborg and participated in NATO exercises in 1957 and 1958, often operating alongside RAF, Dutch and Belgian Hunters from 2nd TAF airfields. In addition, Denmark ordered two Hunter two-seaters similar to the RAF T.7s. They were designated T.53s. The first was flown on 17 October 1958, and both were delivered by the end of the year to Esk-724. Like earlier Danish Hunters, they were fitted with the original wing straight leading edge and were powered by Avon 122

The first production Hunter F.50, 34001, for the Royal Swedish Air Force. (*BAE Systems*)

Line-up of eight Royal Swedish Air Force Hunter F.50s of F9 Wing at Save. (*BAE Systems*)

A well-used Royal Swedish Air Force Hunter F.50, no. 31. (*BAE Systems*)

Four Royal Swedish Air Force Hunter F.50s with F9 Wing at Save. (*BAE Systems*)

engines. Later, in 1968 and 1969, Denmark bought another pair of trainers from the Netherlands. Esk-724 was finally disbanded on 31 March 1974, and in December the next year HSA bought twenty of its aircraft; they were delivered to Dunsfold for refurbishment and possible sale overseas. By this time the Hunter export market had all but dried up and the majority of these aircraft ended up as static museum exhibits.

The success of the Hunter in overseas markets was very much due to its robust construction and flexibility in operation. Of some 2,500 Hunters delivered globally, around 20 per cent were refurbished; many of the early aircraft were conversions of the Belgian and Dutch F.4s. Later conversions included many surplus RAF aircraft, some of which had been used for maintenance training. The refurbishment of F.4s was fairly complex. The fuselage aft of the rear spar needed rebuilding to F.6 standards to accommodate the larger Avon 200 series, although forward of the main spar the fuselage was compatible between all single-seat aircraft. The wings could be fitted with the dog-tooth leading edge, but were otherwise similar, and the tail assembly, flying controls and canopy were identical. Hunters from overseas were usually flown into Dunsfold where they were defueled and made safe before being put into storage on the airfield to await a customer allocation. When ready for the restoration programme, each aircraft was given a survey of its condition, ready to be split into the major components, the tail unit comprising a sixth section. Rear fuselages, wings, ailerons and flaps were shipped to Bitteswell where major jigs were kept, while cockpit canopies and tail surfaces went to Hamble. The Avon engines were returned to Rolls-Royce for overhaul.

On disassembly, the Hunter was stripped of all pipes and cables. Systems such as the hydraulics, pneumatics, oxygen supply and ejection seats were removed and returned to their original manufacturers for reconditioning and recertification. The airframes were stripped down to the primer coat before repainting in the customer's colours. Any damaged wing and fuselage wing skins were removed and replaced—the most common area for damage being the lower wing skin around the main undercarriage pivot point.

The preliminary inspection would have identified the condition of the aircraft and the work required to bring it up to production standard. Each section of the airframe was classified under three headings: 'discard and replace', 'repair' or 'modify'. All sections were identified by a Class B marking to identify them as in the production process, and despite the high level of interchangeability between assemblies, as far as possible all refurbished parts came together as the original Hunter. The main exception was when a single-seat aircraft was converted to a two-seat configuration. In this case the redundant nose was either saved as a spare in the event of damage to an aircraft or it was scrapped. During the refurbishment process, customer-special modifications were incorporated, increasing the overall cost of the finished aircraft. A refurbished Hunter from Dunsfold would have virtually a zero fatigue life, offering a life of some 3,000 flying hours at a fraction of the cost of a more modern and sophisticated combat aircraft. A fully overhauled FGA.9 or FR.10 could cost an air force around £500,000 in the mid-1970s.

Four Royal Danish Air Force Hunter F.51s, including E-410, in formation. (*BAE Systems*)

Royal Danish Air Force Hunter F.51 E-407. (*BAE Systems*)

Royal Danish Air Force Hunter T.53 272. (*BAE Systems*)

Retired Danish Hunter F.51s of Esk-724 in open storage at Dunsfold in February 1978. Many became museum exhibits around Britain. (*Philip Birtles*)

With the South American market usually equipped with surplus US fighters, it came as a surprise when an order was placed by Peru in 1955 for sixteen ex-RAF F.4s. These were designated F.52s, and most had not seen RAF service and therefore had low flying hours. The Hunters for Peru were returned from the RAF to Dunsfold at the end of 1955, where they were refurbished and brought up to the latest modification standard before being painted in the new colours. The first aircraft, 630, was flown on 1 December 1955, and together with other early aircraft, it was used for training Peruvian pilots. Deliveries were made by sea in May 1956 and the aircraft were based at Limatambo and Talara. In 1959 a single Hunter T.62 trainer was ordered by Peru. It was converted from RAF F.4 WT706, and was first flown as 681 on 15 September 1959. By 1968 the Mk 52s were beginning to be replaced by Mirage VPs in the interceptor role; the Hunters, meanwhile, were reallocated to the ground-attack role. Unfortunately they were fitted with the early pre-modification 228 wings which had provision for only two pylons, making them less effective for these duties. In 1976 the Hunters were replaced by Su-22s, although they were retained for operational training.

India placed the first export order for Hunter F.6s in September 1957 for an initial batch of 160 F.56s, all fitted with gun-blast deflectors and tail parachutes. The first thirty-two were already in production for the RAF, but were diverted to India to ensure early deliveries. The sixteen that followed had already been delivered to RAF MUs and were returned to Dunsfold for preparation for India. The forty-ninth aircraft and all those that followed were newly built to the Indian standard. Later aircraft were also modified to carry 230-gallon fuel drop tanks. The first aircraft for India, BA201, first flew on 11 October 1957. It was used for initial training. Deliveries started in November 1957; many were flown by RAF pilots from Benson to India, fitted with four 100-gallon underwing ferry fuel tanks. The Hunters equipped 7, 17, 20 and 27 Squadrons Indian Air Force, based at Ambala and Poona. The final aircraft was flown on 5 October 1960 and delivered in November. This aircraft was the last single-seat Hunter to be built in Britain. The Hunters of the Indian Air Force were involved in combat operations over Portuguese Goa and Northern Frontier disputes with China. Despite being outclassed as interceptors in the 1960s, they were adapted to the ground-attack role, and this resulted in a further order for single-seat Hunters in 1965, and again in 1967 and 1968, amounting to a total of fifty-three additional orders of the aircraft. These were refurbished ex-RAF Hunters and ex-Netherlands Mk 6s, modified for ground-attack duties as Mk 56As.

Within the same basic contract there was provision for sixteen export Hunter two-seater trainers, designated T.66. This version, powered by Avon 203 turbojets and armed with two Aden cannons in fairings under either side of the cockpit, was based on the F.6. The first aircraft, BS361, was first flown on 6 August 1958, before the start of a lengthy period of trials during which new gun-blast deflectors were developed. These trials resulted in a delay in the first delivery until February 1959, when the aircraft were issued to existing Hunter squadrons as operational trainers. A second contract for six T.66s for India was placed in 1960. The final Indian delivery was BS490 in November 1960, the last new Hunter to be built in

Peru Air Force Hunter F.52 638, converted from an ex-RAF F.4. (*BAE Systems*)

Peru Air Force Hunter T.62 681 at Dunsfold prior to delivery. (*BAE Systems*)

Britain, which had first flown on 21 October 1960. With the original T.66s being so effective, a further twelve T.66Ds were ordered in 1966, modified to the latest standard and capable of carrying 230-gallon underwing fuel tanks stressed for ground-attack operations. These refurbished ex-Netherlands F.6s were delivered in 1968. In 1974 a further order was placed for five T.66Es. These were converted from ex-RAF F.6s and all were delivered by December 1973. Each of the four Hunter squadrons operated two trainers, with the balance equipping the OCU at Ambala.

With the conflicts between India and Pakistan in 1965 and 1971, Hunters were in combat against F-86F Sabres, F-104s, MiG-19s and Mirage IIIEs. They did not perform well in air-to-air fighting, but they excelled in the ground-attack role. Some thirteen Hunters were lost in the 1965 conflict and another six in 1971. In the early 1980s, Hashimara-based 20 Squadron formed an aerobatic team known as 'The Thunderbolts'.

In 1963, the Kuwaiti government ordered four Hunter Mk 57s to FGA.9 standard. These aircraft were refurbished ex-Belgian Mk 6s, and deliveries were made from February 1965. Within the same order was a pair of T.67s which were converted from refurbished Belgian F.6s, with three more ordered in 1967, two being ex-Netherlands and one ex-RAF. In 1967 a further order was placed for three more FGA.67s, and two RAF F.6s were transferred the same year. When A-4 Skyhawks were delivered in 1975, the FGA.57s were put into store and later delivered to Oman, while the T.67s continued in service as advanced trainers until retirement.

Indian Air Force Hunter F.56 501. (*BAE Systems*)

Indian Air Force Hunter F.56 511 with underwing rocket pods. (*BAE Systems*)

Indian Air Force Hunter T.66 BS361 at Dunsfold, ready for delivery. (*BAE Systems*)

Indian Air Force Hunter T.66 BS366 in service. (*BAE Systems*)

Indian Air Force Hunter FR.10 512. (*BAE Systems*)

Indian Air Force Hunter F.56 BA469. (*BAE Systems*)

Indian Air Force Hunter F.56 BA312A target tug. (*BAE Systems*)

Indian Air Force Hunter T.66 S573 target tug. (*BAE Systems*)

Kuwaiti Hunter FGA.57 212 at Dunsfold, 1965. (*RAF Museum*)

Kuwaiti Hunter T.67 at Dunsfold, ready for delivery. (*BAE Systems*)

In June and July 1957, two Hunter F.6s, XE587 and XE588, were demonstrated in Switzerland in an international competition for a new day fighter. Characteristics studied were performance, handling and weapons delivery capability. Hawker won the competition and received an order in January 1958 for 100 aircraft based on the F.6; this became the Mk 58 with identities J-4001 to J-4100. Changes from RAF standard included the fitting of Swiss UHF and STR.9X radios, and enlarged link containers to collect the shell cases as well. The first dozen aircraft were refurbished F.6s. J-4001 made its first flight on 29 March 1958, and the whole initial batch was delivered by the end of the year. The remaining F.58s were all new-production and fitted with tail parachutes to cope with landing at some of the limited alpine airfields. Deliveries were completed in April 1960 and issued to 1, 11 and 18 Squadrons, which operated from Dubendorf and Meiringen. A follow-on order for thirty Hunters to FGA.9 standard was placed in 1971. These aircraft came from a variety of sources and were delivered in sub-assemblies to be completed by the Swiss Aircraft Factory at Emmen. They were given the identities J-4101 to J-4130. In 1973 a further order was placed for twenty-two F.58As using ex-RAF F.4s and F.6s. Again these were completed at Emmen and given the serial range J-4131 to J-4152. The final Swiss order was for four ex-RAF F.4s and four ex-Swedish Mk 50s to be converted by HSA to two-seat trainers with Avon 207 engines, designated T.68s. They were given serials J-4201 to J-4208 and were delivered between August 1974 and June 1975.

The Swiss F.58As and T.68s were operated by 4, 5, 7, 8, 19 and 21 Squadrons. In 1982 the Hunter 80 programme, what is now known as a mid-life improvement programme, began. It included a comprehensive update of newly developed weapons and systems. Provision was made for carrying Maverick air-to-ground missiles on inboard wing pylons, and defences were improved by the addition of chaff/flare

The first Swiss Hunter F.58, J-4001, at Dunsfold awaiting delivery. This aircraft first flew on 27 January 1956 as XE536, and was delivered to 5 MU on 23 February. It returned to Dunsfold on 20 January 1958 and was converted to F.58 configuration, flying again on 13 March 1959. This was followed by its delivery to Emmen on 3 April. It served with 7 and 20 Staffel and was AIM-9 configured in 1964. On 16 December 1994 it became the last Swiss Hunter to fly operationally, with 2,541 hours and 1,330 landings completed. It was preserved in the Fliegermusem at Dubendorf from August 2002. (*BAE Systems*)

Swiss Hunter F.58A J-4023 at Dubendorf in August 1983. This aircraft was first flown on 21 February 1959 and delivered to Kloten on 10 March, joining 20 Staffel on 4 April. This Hunter served for a while with the Patrouille Suisse and finally retired on 4 May 1994 with a total of 2,869 hours and 1,567 landings, the highest of all Swiss Hunters. It was broken up at Meiringen. (*Philip Birtles*)

Swiss Hunter F.58 J-4088 at Lugano Air Show in June 1973. This Hunter first flew on 9 December 1959 and was delivered to Emmen on 21 January 1960, entering service with 21 Staffel on 3 February. It was modified to carry the AIM-9 Sidewinder and AGM-65 Maverick, but was destroyed in a mid-air collision with J-4113 on 17 October 1984 during ground-attack training at Bonoduz. (*Philip Birtles*)

Swiss Hunter F.58A J-4150 at Dubendorf in August 1983. This Hunter was part of the third contract and was converted from XF312. With the RAF this aircraft was originally delivered to 5 MU on 18 January 1956 and served with 71, 112 and 26 Squadrons, following which it was used for ground instruction as 7848M. It was returned to HAL in June 1972 and converted to FGA.9 standard as an F.58A, with delivery to the Swiss Air Force on 19 September 1975. It was modified for AIM-9 air-to-air missile operation and finally retired to Interlaken on 3 December 1991 and broken up. (*Philip Birtles*)

Swiss Hunter T.68 J-4203 on approach to Emmen in September 1980. This two-seat Hunter first flew as WV398, an F.4, on 29 August 1955. It was delivered to the RAF on 19 September 1955 and served with 20 and 26 Squadrons, followed by 229 OCU, before becoming 7767M. It was acquired by HAL in January 1973 as G-9-411 and converted to T.68, with a surface delivery in March 1975 for assembly in Switzerland. It was delivered to 24 Staffel on 26 February 1976 and also served with 5 Staffel. The aircraft was modified to carry AIM-9s on the outer port pylon and a chaff/flare pod under the other wing. It was retired from military service on 16 December 1994 and made a last military flight into storage at Raron. It was moved to the Musée de l'Aviation Militaire de Payerne, where it was restored to fly on 18 May 2004 as HB-RVW. It made its final flight on 3 October 2014 and is now a static exhibit. (*Philip Birtles*)

dispensers in the rear of the link/shell case collectors as well as a radar warning antenna on either side of the nose cone. In addition, in 1994 the internationally renowned 'Patrouille Suisse' aerobatic team celebrated their thirty years of Hunter operations. The team made its first public display with four Hunters on 2 June 1959 with varying formation flypasts. In 1963, the team became fully aerobatic and was given official status on 22 August 1964. In 1970 a fifth Hunter was added and in 1978 the team gave their first international display with the addition of a sixth Hunter. The team continued with international displays, often at the RIAT at Fairford, until their last show with Hunters on 25 September 1994. After this the Hunters were replaced by F-5s, and by the end of the year they had been retired from service in Switzerland.

A batch of fifteen ex-RAF F.6s were evaluated by the Iraqi Air Force in 1958 and '59. They formed a squadron based at Habbaniyah with pilots trained at 229 OCU at Chivenor. As a result of good experience with the Hunters, orders were placed in 1963 for twenty-four FGA.9s. In 1965 a further order was placed for eighteen more FGA.9-standard aircraft, designated Mk 59 and 59A, plus four FR.10s designated Mk 59Bs, making a total of forty-six Hunters. The aircraft were refurbished Belgian Hunters. Three trainers were converted from Belgian F.6s for delivery in 1963 and 1964, and two more trainers were delivered in 1965. The Iraqi Air Force used Hunters to tackle local tribal uprisings as well as in both the 1967 Six-Day War and the 1973 Yom Kippur War. By the time war broke out with Iran, the Hunters had been relegated to training duties with the OCU.

Patrouille Suisse Hunter F.58As in earlier camouflage markings. (*Philip Birtles*)

Patrouille Suisse Hunter F.58As at Boscombe Down Air Show in June 1992 in latest colours. (*Philip Birtles*)

Patrouille Suisse Hunter F.58A J-4026 at Boscombe Down in June 1992. This Hunter first flew on 4 March 1959 and was delivered to Emmen on 3 April, joining 20 Staffel on 24 April 1959. It was configured for AIM-9 in 1964 and served with the Patrouille Suisse until retiring on 28 November 1994 at Emmen. It was flown to Basle on 30 May 1995 to join a private collection. (*Philip Birtles*)

Swiss Hunter F.58A J-4022 at Fairford in July 1994 at a celebration of thirty years of the Patrouille Suisse aerobatic team, and the last with the Hunter. This Hunter first flew on 19 February 1959 and was delivered to Emmen on 2 April. It was configured for AIM-9 in 1964 and joined the Patrouille Suisse. It was retired on 16 December 1994 at Emmen. It was flown to Dubendorf on 11 July 1995, and then departed for the Szolnok Museum in Hungary on 27 July 1995. (*Philip Birtles*)

Swiss Hunter F.58 J-4007 in smart blue/yellow livery, carrying an underwing AGM-65 Maverick missile. (*BAE Systems*)

Swiss Hunter F.58 J-4013, used for missile development with a recording camera in its gun pod. (*BAE Systems*)

Swiss Air Force Hunter F.58s deployed on a typical airfield surrounded by mountains. (*BAE Systems*)

Hunter F.59s for Iraq await delivery at Dunsfold. (*BAE Systems*)

Iraqi Air Force Hunter F.59s ready to go from Dunsfold. (*BAE Systems*)

An Iraqi Air Force Hunter FGA.59. (*BAE Systems*)

A Hunter F.56 with the Iraqi Air Force at RAF Habbaniya, September 1956. (*RAF Museum*)

An Iraqi Air Force Hunter T.73. (*BAE Systems*)

Hunter F.6 XG236 of 66 Squadron on loan to the Iraqi Air Force. (*BAE Systems*)

In February 1962, the Royal Rhodesian Air Force (RRAF) ordered twelve ex-RAF Hunter F.6s to be modified to full FGA.9 standard. Deliveries arrived in December 1963, equipping 1 Squadron at Thornhill. With the unilateral declaration of independence (UDI) in 1965, followed by the proclamation of a republic in 1969, the Hunters became part of the Rhodesian Air Force (RhAF). During the 1970s, they were used in ground-attack duties against rebel forces in Angola, Botswana, Mozambique and Zambia, despite all spares and support being embargoed from Britain. During these engagements only two aircraft were lost to enemy action. Following elections in 1979, a black-majority government came to power and the country was renamed Zimbabwe. The Hunters became part of the Zimbabwe Air Force (ZAF), which added four Hunter FGA.80s from Kenya to their fleet. On 25 July 1982, several Hunters were destroyed on the ground during a sabotage attack at Thornhill, and by 1987 the survivors had been replaced by Chinese MiG-21s.

The most famous Hunter in the early 1960s was the Hawker demonstrator Mk 66A G-APUX. Spinning a swept-wing jet fighter was usually avoided, especially after a T.7 was lost in an inverted spin. As a result, a comprehensive spinning programme was undertaken by A. W. 'Bill' Bedford; it was so successful that at both the 1959 and 1960 SBAC Farnborough displays, Bill demonstrated twelve turn spins from 15,000 feet over the airfield. They were made visible to the public

Hunter FGA.9 116, one of the batch for the Royal Rhodesian Air Force. (*BAE Systems*)

Royal Rhodesian Air Force Hunter FGA.9 125 taxiing. (*BAE Systems*)

by the injection of diesel oil in the jet exhaust, which created a smoke trail. G-APUX had been built using a badly damaged Belgian Air Force F.6, which had made a wheels-up forced landing. During repairs at Kingston, an ex-Indian Air Force two-seat T.66 nose was fitted in place of the original single-seat forward fuselage. Powered by a 10,050-lb-thrust Avon 207, the aircraft had two 30-mm Aden cannons fitted, and unlike other T.7s, it featured a Dunlop nosewheel brake with Maxaret anti-skid. This reduced the landing run to 1,500 feet. A 13-foot-6-inch-diameter brake parachute replaced the standard one of 10 feet 6 inches.

G-APUX had been perfectly rigged and trimmed for spinning tests, and Bill Bedford called it 'the sweetest Hunter I have had the pleasure to fly'. In 1960 it was used to test a pair of extra large 350-gallon fuel drop tanks to give an increased ferry range. The tanks were built by adding a 3-foot section to the standard 230-gallon tanks, thus extending the length. The tank was braced by a strut to the wing and was stressed to 7 g for use during long-range ground-attack missions. However, these tanks were never carried by production Hunters.

G-APUX was later flown from the RAE at Farnborough on Rank Cintel Peep head-up display development. After a return to Hawker, the aircraft was leased to the Iraqi Air Force, pending delivery of their two T.69s, and on return from lease, it was loaned to the Lebanese and Jordanian Air Forces, returning to Dunsfold on 18 December 1965. In August 1967 it was finally sold as one of four T.72s for the Chilean Air Force with the designation Mk 72.

The Lebanese Air Force received its first Hunters in 1958 when six ex-RAF F.6s were transferred, financed by US offshore funds. Three Hunter T.66Cs were ordered by Lebanon in 1964. They were refurbished ex-Belgian F.6s, one of which

Hawker demonstrator Hunter T.66 G-APUX, fitted with long-range ferry underwing fuel tanks. (*BAE Systems*)

Hunter T.66 G-APUX alongside Trident 1 G-ARPB, while waiting for the demonstration of both types at Farnborough Air Show in September 1962. (*Philip Birtles*)

A Hawker Hunter T.66 displaying at Farnborough Air Show. (*BAE Systems*)

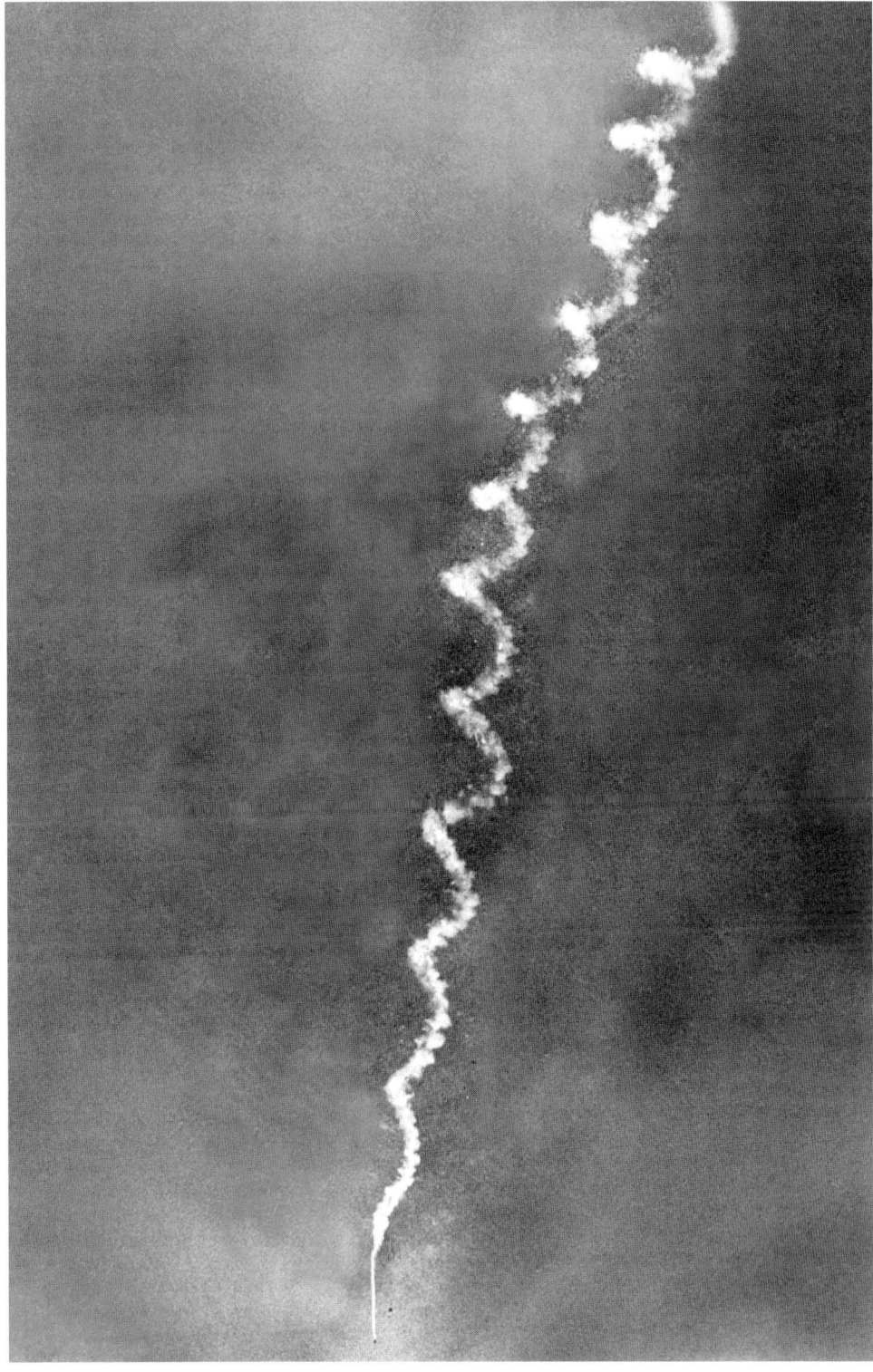

Twelve turns of a spin by Bill Bedford in Hunter T.66 G-APUX at Farnborough Air Show. (*BAE Systems*)

Lebanese Air Force Hunter FGA.70 L178 at Dunsfold. (*BAE Systems*)

A Lebanese Air Force Hunter FGA.70 in Lebanon. (*BAE Systems*)

Lebanese Air Force Hunter T.66C L286. (*BAE Systems*)

replaced the leased G-APUX. Later, another four ex-Belgian F.6s, refurbished to full FGA.9 standard and designated Mk 70, were ordered by Lebanon. Deliveries were completed in September 1966. To replace losses inflicted by Israel, an additional six ex-RAF Hunters were supplied in 1975–76. These consisted of an F.6, three FGA.9s and two FR.10s. The eventual total was nineteen Hunters. Some continued to operate in Lebanon until the late 1980s.

Chile placed an order for fifteen single-seat ex-Netherlands and Belgian Hunters in 1966 after protracted negotiations, with strong competition from the USA. Deliveries were completed by 1968. To these FGA.71s were added three FR.10s. A follow-on order of nine more FGA.9s was delivered by September 1971, and a third order for four FGA.9s was completed in January 1974. Two contracts were then placed for a total of six FR.10s, followed by two further contracts for a total of six two-seat T.72s. Deliveries were completed by February 1974. Among the trainers were the refurbished XJ627 and the famous G-APUX. All the Chilean Hunters were powered by 10,000-lb-thrust Avon 207s. The Hunter fleet was based with Grupos de Aviacion No. 8 at Antofagasta in the north of Chile. Unfortunately, due to political criticism within the British government, an embargo was put on the supply of spares for the Chilean Hunters from 1974 to 1980, resulting in a rapid decline in serviceability, with only twenty remaining operational by 1978. The loss of capability was rapidly filled by assistance from the USA, Argentina and Brazil. After 1980, when spares were again available, the Hunters were updated with radar warning receivers, chaff/flare dispensers and US cockpit instrumentation. They were also given provision for carrying the Israeli Shafrir air-to-air missile.

A Hunter T.72 for Chile at Dunsfold. (*BAE Systems*)

Chilean Air Force Hunter FGA.71 722. (*BAE Systems*)

Chilean Air Force Hunter FGA.71 724 with Shafrir missile firing. (*BAE Systems*)

Chilean Air Force Hunter FGA.71 715 top sides. (*BAE Systems*)

Chilean Air Force Hunter T.72 J-718, ready for delivery from Dunsfold. (*RAF Museum*)

In 1958, twelve ex-RAF Hunter F.6s were supplied to the Royal Jordanian Air Force (RJAF) by the British government, equipping 1 Squadron based at Mafraq. A year later, Jordan ordered direct from HSA three Hunter trainers based on the Indian Mk 66Bs. These were delivered in 1960. The first aircraft was from the Kingston production line and the second and third were refurbished ex-Netherlands F.6s, the second one replacing the leased G-APUX. Also in 1960 and 1961, a pair of ex-RAF FR.10s were transferred to the RJAF. In the early 1960s an aerobatic team called 'The Hashemite Diamonds' was formed for local 'in-country' displays. In 1962, 2 Squadron was formed with the transfer of a further twelve Hunters from the RAF, later to be increased by eight ex-RAF F.6s converted to FGA.9 standard, becoming Mk 73s. At the start of the Six-Day War in 1967, the Israeli Air Force destroyed the only Jordanian early warning radar installation, and by the end of the conflict, only two Hunters were left intact. As replacements, Saudi Arabia gave Jordan three single-seat Hunters in 1968. Four FGA.9s were also transferred from the RAF, and four ex-RAF F.6s were ordered to the FGA.9 configuration from HSA as Mk 73As. This was followed by a second order for eight Mk 73As, and then a third order for three more of the same mark. By June 1972 the Jordanian Air Force had a strength of thirty-five single-seat and three two-seat Hunters. They were scheduled for retirement when the Yom Kippur War started in 1973. This delayed their replacement until 1975, when Abu Dhabi presented King Hussein of Jordan with twelve Hunters, which joined nineteen Jordanian survivors. Later in the same year, King Hussein donated all of his thirty-one Hunters to the Sultan of Oman.

Royal Jordanian Air Force Hunter FGA.73A 845 outside the assembly hangar at Dunsfold in August 1971. It was converted from RAF F.4 WV408. (*Philip Birtles*)

Royal Jordanian Air Force Hunter FR.10 712 at Dunsfold prior to delivery. (*BAE Systems*)

A Royal Jordanian Air Force Hunter FGA.73. (*BAE Systems*)

Royal Jordanian Air Force Hunter T.66B 800 with full overload fuel tanks on a damp day at Dunsfold, with surplus Hunters and Sea Furies in the background. (*BAE Systems*)

Royal Jordanian Air Force Hunter FGA.73s at Luqa in Malta, 28 July 1972, on delivery to Jordan. (*BAE Systems*)

The Sultan of Oman's Air Force was formed with British support on 1 March 1959 with headquarters at Muscat. Following Britain's withdrawal from Aden, Chinese and Soviet influence began to destabilise the region. Britain responded by offering Oman a considerable number of Hunters without involving HSA. A number of ex-RAF Persian Gulf-operated Hunter FGA.9s were transferred to Oman; these, along with the ex-Kuwaiti Mk 57s and Jordanian Mk 73s, gave 6 Squadron at Thumrayt base a total of thirty-one Hunters. A number of these Hunters were only suitable for spares support, however.

Having gained independence from the Federation of Malaysia in 1965, the Republic of Singapore ordered sixteen refurbished ex-RAF Hunter F.6s in July 1968: twelve configured as FGA.9s and four FR.10s, with the designations Mk 74 and 74A. These aircraft were delivered in 1970 and 1971 to 140 (Osprey) Squadron based at Tengah. The pilots were responsible for local air defence, army co-operation and tactical reconnaissance. The Hunters were regularly armed with SNEB Matra rocket batteries under the outboard wing pylons and were equipped with 230-gallon fuel drop tanks inboard to give a practical endurance. Over the next two years, further orders were placed for twenty-two Mk 74B single-seat Hunter FR.10s. These came from eight ex-RAF Mk 4s and fourteen ex-RAF Mk 6s. In addition, nine two-seat T.75As and 75Bs were ordered, with deliveries completed by October 1973. With the addition of these later aircraft, a second 141 (Merlin) Squadron was formed with Hunters armed with Sidewinder air-to-air missiles. The Republic of Singapore Air Force (RSAF) was formed on 1 April 1975 and many of the forty-seven Hunters continued in service well into the 1980s.

A Sultan of Oman Air Force Hunter FGA.9. (*BAE Systems*)

A Sultan of Oman Air Force Hunter FR.10 over the desert. (*BAE Systems*)

A Sultan of Oman Air Force Hunter FGA.9 on patrol. (*BAE Systems*)

Singapore Hunter FGA.74 533. (*BAE Systems*)

Singapore Air Force Hunter FGA.74 534. (*BAE Systems*)

As the RAF began its progressive withdrawal from the Middle East, the independence of the Trucial States came under threat, precipitating the need for an effective air-defence capability. With their proven record and acceptable price tag, the Hunters were an obvious choice. An order was placed by Abu Dhabi in 1969 for seven FGA.76s and three FR.76As. The aircraft supplied were refurbished ex-RAF F.4s and F.6s, and included in the contract were two refurbished ex-Netherlands trainers, designated T.77. The Hunters formed a ground-attack squadron in 1970, based at the former RAF base of Sharjah.

Qatar placed an order for three FGA.78s in June 1969. Two of these aircraft were converted ex-Netherlands F.6s, and one was a two-seat ex-Netherlands T.7, delivered in 1970 as a T.79. The aircraft were used for combat air patrols off the Qatar coastline from the base at Doha. They had fully modified 228 standard wings and therefore provision for four underwing 230-gallon fuel tanks.

Four ex-RAF Hunter F.6s were delivered to the Royal Saudi Air Force in May 1966 for border protection and to give the RSAF pilots the lead in training for the English Electric Lightnings. All were delivered in May 1966. With the arrival of the first Lightnings in 1967, the Hunters were withdrawn, and three survivors were passed to the Royal Jordanian Air Force in 1968. Also as part of the 'Magic Carpet' defence contract with Saudi Arabia, two ex-RAF Hunter T.7s, XL605 and XL620, were delivered in May 1966. These two aircraft were presented to Jordan in 1968, and returned to the UK in 1974 when they were redelivered to the RAF as XX467 and XX466. XX467 is now preserved at the Newark Air Museum.

Abu Dhabi Air Force Hunter FGA.76 702. (*BAE Systems*)

Abu Dhabi Air Force Hunter FGA.76 701. (*RAF Museum*)

Abu Dhabi Air Force Hunter T.66 711. (*BAE Systems*)

Qatar Air Force FGA.78. (*BAE Systems*)

Royal Saudi Air Force Hunter F.6 60-602 at Dunsfold. (*BAE Systems*)

Royal Saudi Air Force Hunter T.7 70-616. (*BAE Systems*)

Royal Saudi Air Force Hunter F.60 60-602. (*BAE Systems*)

Royal Saudi Air Force Hunter F.60 60-602. (*RAF Museum*)

After Kenya gained its independence in 1963, the British government helped equip the Kenya Air Force, which formed in June 1964. Initial equipment consisted of a pair of Chipmunks followed by Beavers and Caribou. The country's new-found independence was threatened by neighbouring countries Ethiopia, Somalia and Uganda, which prompted an order for six Strikemasters in 1970. To increase their defensive capability, Kenya became the final customer for refurbished Hunters, ordering six aircraft in 1974. These consisted of four FGA.80s, converted from three ex-RAF F.4s and one FR.10, plus a pair of ex-FAA T.8s, designated T.81s. Delivery started with the trainers and one Mk 80 on 24 June 1974, and the last delivery was made on 13 January 1975. The Hunters operated until 1979, by which time only four were airworthy. They were replaced by F-5s, and the Hunters went into storage until they were bought by Zimbabwe and based at Thornhill.

In addition to the Hunter production lines at Kingston, Blackpool and Coventry, there was licensed production in Belgium and the Netherlands. With the early development of the Cold War and the military might of the Warsaw Pact—which included the introduction of the MiG-15—NATO front-line defences, consisting of Vampires, Venoms, Meteors and some F-84 Thunderjets, were deemed inadequate. The start of the Korean War on 25 June 1950 created the need for new fighter development and production on a scale that European countries could ill afford. However, the US government passed the Offshore Procurement Bill (OSP), which provided funds to finance the necessary development and production.

On 10 July 1952, prototype WB188 was flown by Neville Duke to the Brussels Air Show to promote the Hawker Hunter for the NATO requirement. This was followed on 22 October 1952 by the arrival of a USAF evaluation team at Dunsfold; both WB188 and WB195 were flown by USAF pilots with glowing results. Although the Hunter missed out on the original OSP orders in April 1952, a second group of contracts placed in April 1953 covered Hunters for the RAF and for production under licence in Europe for NATO air forces. The initial OSP contracts covered sixty-four Hunters to be built in Belgium and forty-eight in the Netherlands. These were F.4s with provision for a pair of pylon-mounted wing fuel drop tanks and with the two rear fuselage tanks replaced by fuel bag tanks located in the wings. While OSP funding allowed production lines to be established, both countries increased the orders with local government funding, leading to their acquisition of later marks.

In Belgium, a total of 112 Hunters equivalent to the RAF F.4s were built by Avions Fairey, Brussels, and SABCA during 1955–56. They were numbered ID-1 onwards, and served with 1, 7 and 9 Wings at Beauvechain, Chirvres and Bierset. The same factories produced 144 Hunter F.6s between 1956 and 1958. These were numbered IF-1 onwards, and were operated by 7 and 9 Wings. The Belgian Air Force formed 'Le Diables Rouges' (The Red Devils) aerobatic team, and from 1957 to 1965 they flew a formation of five Hunter F.6s, painted overall red. After service with the Belgian Air Force, many of the Hunters were put into storage due to poor serviceability. HSA bought ninety-four back at scrap value for refurbishment and overseas sale. Although a further payment was made from the profits made by HSA, it was only a token and there were some hard feelings on the part of the Belgian factories.

Kenya Air Force Hunter T.81 801 at Malta, on its delivery flight to Kenya. (*BAE Systems*)

Kenya Air Force Hunter FGA.80 805, 1974. (*RAF Museum*)

Belgian Air Force Hunter F.4 ID-107 7JO. (*BAE Systems*)

Belgian Hunter F.6 IF-70 of Le Diables Rouges aerobatic team, 1962. (*Newark Air Museum*)

Belgian Air Force Hunter F.4 ID-46 F-7J. (*BAE Systems*)

Belgian Air Force Hunter F.4 IF-21 IS-X. (*BAE Systems*)

Belgian Air Force Hunter F.4 IF-124. (*BAE Systems*)

Belgian Air Force Hunter F.4 IF-60 060. (*BAE Systems*)

In the Netherlands, Fokker built a total of ninety-six Hunters similar to RAF F.4s in 1955–56. They were numbered N-101 onwards. They equipped 324 and 325 Squadrons at Leeuwarden and 327 Squadron at Soesterberg. None were bought by HSA. Fokker also built ninety-three F.6 RAF equivalents between 1956 and 1958, with numbering starting at N-201. These aircraft served with the Netherlands Air Force from 1957 to 1963, and initially replaced the earlier F.4s, which were operated by 322, 323, 324, 325, 326 and 327 Squadrons. From 1963, all but 325 Squadron, which flew Hunters until 1966, had their Hunters replaced by F-104s. From February 1964 to August 1968, forty-seven Hunters were bought by HSA for refurbishment and sale overseas.

In addition to using locally produced Hunters, the Netherlands ordered twenty T.7s from Kingston. The first ten were numbered N-301 to N-310, and the next ten were built from a cancelled MOS batch and numbered N-311 to N-320. Power was from the Avon 121A, and a tail parachute was fitted. Armament consisted of a single Aden cannon. First flight of N-301 was on 19 March 1958 and deliveries were made between 18 July 1958 and 4 February 1959. The two-seat Hunters served with the operational conversion unit based at Twente, and ten of these trainers were bought back by HSA for overseas sales.

Royal Netherlands Air Force Hunter F.4 N-268. (*BAE Systems*)

Royal Netherlands Air Force Hunter F.4 N-143 3P-4. (*BAE Systems*)

The first Royal Netherlands Air Force Hunter T.7, N-301. (*BAE Systems*)

Royal Netherlands Air Force Hunter T.7 N-302. (*BAE Systems*)

CC-705, one of about five ex-Rhodesian Air Force Hunter FGA.9s operated by the Somali Air Force from around 1990 to 1993. (*BAE Systems*)

A Somali Hunter FGA.9 with T.7 CC711, *c*. 1993. (*BAE Systems*)

Hunter FGA.74B G-BABM at Farnborough in September 1972, celebrating export successes before its delivery to Singapore. This aircraft was previously RAF FGA.9 XF432. (*Philip Birtles*)

9

The Jet Set

With the retirement of Hunters from the RAF, Swiss and other air forces, there was no longer a market for examples refurbished at Kingston, but there were still a number of airframes available in good condition with relatively low flying hours. While some were allocated to aviation museums, others were bought by enthusiasts to fly and for the public to enjoy.

The first of these enthusiasts was Spencer Flack. He bought ex-Danish Hunter F.4 E-418 from Dunsfold and had it restored in an overall red scheme as G-HUNT, to add to his similarly painted Spitfire and Sea Fury. Spencer later added to his collection a two-seat Hunter, G-BOOM, painted in similar livery.

G-HUNT had made its first flight as E-418 on 22 June 1956. In 1975, after retirement, it was flown back to Dunsfold where it was stored in the open, together with a number of other ex-Danish Hunters. It was then restored to fly by Eric Hayward at Hurn for Spencer Flack, and made its post-restoration flight on 20 March 1980. It was based with Jet Heritage at Hurn from September 1981 until 1987, and sold to Houston, Texas, as N50972 in December 1987. It went to the Combat Jets Flying Museum from February 1988 to 1992, when it moved to the Air Venture Museum as N611JR. It is last recorded as being part of the collection at Classic Aircraft Aviation Museum in Oregon in 2009, where it is probably on static display.

The two-seat G-BOOM was built by Fokker in the Netherlands as N-307, and made its first flight on 20 September 1958. After Spencer Flack, it was bought by Mike Carlton at the Jet Heritage Museum at Hurn. Upon Carlton's death, it was acquired by the Royal Jordanian Historic Flight, and was flown to Jordan to be based there.

With the release from service of the FAA and Swiss Hunters, more good aircraft were available for private ownership. Hunter Flying, a company based at Exeter, specialised in Hunter engineering and restoring aircraft to airworthy status. They did this for a number of private owners and were also involved in rebuilding aircraft for Hawker Hunter Aviation at Scampton and Northern Lights in Canada. Some of these rebuilds involved converting single-seat Hunters to a two-seat configuration. Delta Jets at Kemble also had CAA approval to restore,

Ex-Danish Hunter F.4 E-418 at Dunsfold, February 1978. (*Philip Birtles*)

Spencer Flack's red Hunter Mk 4 G-HUNT at Mildenhall, May 1981. (*Philip Birtles*)

Spencer Flack's red Hunter T.7 G-BOOM at Finningley, September 1993. (*Philip Birtles*)

Jordanian Hunter T.7 800F of 1 Squadron, ex-G-BOOM, at Hurn, July 1994. (*Philip Birtles*)

maintain and fly Hunters for their owners, and they increased their profile by organising jet heritage air displays for the benefit of the public.

Barry Pover of the Lightning Flying Club (LFC) bought GA.11 XE685 at auction in 1994 and registered it G-GAII, based at Exeter. His overriding passion was to restore a Lightning to fly on the civil register, but he was unable to convince the CAA that it was safe. Hunter F.4 XE685 was built at the Blackpool factory and delivered to 33 MU at RAF Lyneham on 18 July 1955. It served with both 93 and 98 Squadrons at Jever in RAF Germany, and was later replaced by the newer F.6. After a period of storage, the Royal Navy acquired the airframe and it was converted by Hawker to the GA.11 configuration for delivery to 738 NAS at Lossiemouth on 6 May 1963. It moved with the squadron to Brawdy in December 1963, and in early 1965 it joined 764 NAS back at Lossiemouth. From October 1966 until July 1968, XE685 was loaned to Hawker Aircraft for practice bomb and RP trials, after which it returned to Lossiemouth. On 27 February 1969, the aircraft joined the Yeovilton Station Flight, returning to 764 NAS at Lossiemouth in 1972. The Hunter then joined the Air Director Training Unit (ADTU) back at Yeovilton in October 1972, which became the Fleet Requirements and Air Director School (FRADU). XE685 was finally retired from military use on 30 March 1994.

The LFC became the Classic Jet Aircraft Company and G-GAII made regular appearances at air shows from 1995 to 1998. In 1999 the aircraft was stored at RAF St Mawgan and then was handed between a number of different owners until it finally flew again from Exeter on 11 February 2006. After that date the aircraft appeared at several air displays. In 2010 it was acquired by its fifth civilian owner as part of a four-Hunter display team known as 'Team Viper'. They operated a busy display schedule in 2011 before disbanding in early 2012. XE685 was then bought by Scampton-based Hawker Hunter Aviation (HHA) and is now (2022) being maintained in flying condition, pending the award of a suitable contract.

Kemble, the base for the Hunter 5 MU, became a Hunter haven, with maintenance and engineering by Delta Jets and air shows every year. The Kemble Hunters included ex-FAA GA.11s and a number of two-seat versions. Hunter GA.11 WV256 first flew on 5 May 1955 and was delivered on 20 May to the RAF. It served with 26 Squadron, and then 229 OCU. Having returned to Hawker in 1960, WV256 was converted to a GA.11 and was delivered on 2 April 1963 to 738 NAS at Lossiemouth. The squadron moved to Brawdy in December 1963, and WV256 later returned to Lossiemouth to join 764 NAS in 1969 until it disbanded in July 1972. It then joined ADS at Yeovilton in 1973, becoming part of FRADU. It was retired from military duties in 1995 and was stored at Shawbury. Having been bought by Barry Pearson at auction in 2000, WV256 became G-BZPB. Based at Exeter, it was restored and flew again in May 2001 and at air shows in 2001 and 2002, when it was painted to represent the original prototype, WB188. Its permit to fly expired in 2003 and it did not fly again. The Hunter was then moved by road to Kemble and was used for spares and static displays at air shows there. In late May 2010 it was moved to Airbase at Coventry, and two years later

Hunter GA.11 G-GAII, ex-XE685, at Exeter, March 1995. (*Philip Birtles*)

Hunter GA.11 XE685 861, ex-FRADU, at Kemble, June 2011. (*Philip Birtles*)

Hunter GA.11 WV256 'WB188' G-BZPB at Kemble, June 2009. (*Philip Jeremiah*)

it went to the new Airbase location at St Mawgan, which is now the Cornwall Aviation Heritage Centre. There the aircraft was returned to its 26 Squadron markings.

Hunter WT723 was part of the first production batch of F.4s and first flew on 16 February 1955, with delivery to 5 MU in March. It served with 54 and 14 Squadrons, followed by 229 OCU. WT723 was then converted to a GA.11 by Hawker and delivered on 17 August 1962 to /64 NAS. A PR camera nose was also fitted at this stage. In 1973 WT723 was delivered to FRADU at Yeovilton, where it was retired after twenty years of flying. The aircraft was then allocated to Culdrose School of Aircraft Handling for training, and later, in 1996, sold to an American and overhauled by Classic Jet Aircraft at Exeter ready for transport to the US. The American sale fell through and WT723 was registered G-PRII for Classic Fighters in Belgium. In 2002 the company ceased to exist and the Hunter was grounded. A new owner bought it and, in 2008, Hunter Flying at Exeter returned it to the air in Black Arrows markings as the lead Hunter XG194 at the Farnborough Air Show, to celebrate the fiftieth anniversary of the twenty-two-Hunter loop at Farnborough. After a brief period with the Kemble-based Team Viper, WT723 moved to St Athan with Hunter Flying.

Like all other aircraft of this mark, Hunter GA.11 XE689 was converted from an F.4, having been delivered to the RAF on 22 July 1955. It had served with 67 and 234 Squadrons before being bought by Hawker in 1961. After conversion to GA.11 configuration, it was delivered to 764 NAS in July 1963. While at this squadron, a Harley light nose was fitted. A move was made to Yeovilton in 1973, where it joined Airwork-operated FRADU. It was finally retired from military service in 1994 and stored at Shawbury. It was bought at auction in 1995 by Exeter-based Classic Jet Aircraft and displayed in 2000. As with many other

Hunter PR.11 WT723 G-PRII, painted as F.6 XG194 N of 111 Squadron, at Kemble, June 2011. (*Philip Birtles*)

Hunter GA.11 XE689 864 G-BWGK at Kemble, July 2008. (*Philip Birtles*)

Exeter-based aircraft, XE689 was moved to Kemble in 2006 as a spares source. When Delta Jets closed down, it was moved to Coventry and then scrapped, although the nose section was preserved and taken to Stroud.

Hunter F.4 XF300 was delivered to 5 MU at Kemble on 9 January 1956, and served with 234 and 130 Squadrons in the RAF. It was returned to Hawker for conversion to a GA.11 and delivered to 738 NAS at Lossiemouth on 12 February 1963. It moved to Brawdy with the squadron and then joined 746 NAS back at Lossiemouth. It was stored in the late 1970s and returned to service on 6 March with FRADU at Yeovilton until its withdrawal in May 1995 for storage at Shawbury. It was sold to Barry Pearson in November 2000. At that stage XF300 left Shawbury and was registered G-BZPC. It was painted in the overall red scheme of F.3 WB188, with the intention of re-enacting the speed record for the fiftieth anniversary in September 2003. Unfortunately, in the event, the aircraft had not achieved airworthy status by the anniversary and a T.8 was substituted. G-BZPC remained on the ground in external storage at Exeter before being moved to Delta Jets at Kemble in 2006. While being assessed for restoration, it was decided that there was too much corrosion in the cockpit. It was used in static line-ups at Kemble and as gate guard for Delta Jets until they closed. The red-painted Hunter left Kemble in late 2011 and is now on external display at the Riverside MOT Centre in Melksham, commemorating the original prototype being on the RAF Melksham gate from 1961 to 1964.

One of the most frequently seen Hunters on the air show circuit was FGA.9 XE601. It was built in 1956 as an F.6 and retained by Hawker for development flying. Following this it was converted to an F.6A and delivered to the A&AEE at Boscombe Down where it served for forty-two years. For its final role it was fitted with large underwing tanks fitted with spray nozzles to provide ground troops with a realistic training experience of chemical and biological attacks from the air. Following retirement in 1999, XE601 was loaned to the Boscombe Down Museum, and put up for tender in 2004. Initially acquired by a Canadian collector but transferred to Skyblue Aviation, XE601 was restored to flying by the Hunter Flying Club. It flew again as G-ETPS on 21 June 2005 and lastly with Team Viper. It was then grounded at Waddington for an engine change that was never completed. The aircraft was acquired by Apache Aviation in France as a spares source, and so is unlikely to fly again.

Although not one of the Kemble residents, Hunter F.6A XF515 had served with 43 Squadron from 1957 until 1964. After RAF service, the aircraft was overhauled by Kennet Aviation at Cranfield and flown as G-KAXF at the Cranfield Classic Jets Show in September 1998. The owner and pilot was Rod Dean, who had flown the same aircraft with 43 Squadron while serving in the RAF. In late 2004, when Mr Dean retired from flying, the aircraft was grounded, bringing a pause to its career in displaying. It was bought by a Dutch collector and flown to Exeter in September 2007 for overhaul by Hunter Flying, where it was given the markings N-294. In late 2008 it was flown from Exeter to its new base at Leeuwarden, and although operating in Europe, it did visit the Waddington Air Show in July 2014.

Hunter FGA.9 XF516 was based at Exeter as G-BVVC and had served with 229 OCU 234 Squadron at Chivenor before becoming ground instruction airframe

Hunter GA.11 XF300, painted as WB188, G-BZPC at Kemble, June 2009. (*Philip Birtles*)

Hunter F.6A XE601, ex-A&AEE, at Kemble, June 2011. (*Philip Birtles*)

Hunter F.6A XF515, painted as R of 43 Squadron, G-KAXF at Fairford, July 1999. (*Philip Birtles*)

Hunter F.6A N-294, ex-XF515, at Waddington, July 2014. (*Philip Birtles*)

8885M. It appeared at a number of air displays including the Farnborough Air Show, and was registered to the Chivenor Memorial Flight. On 1 June the aircraft departed Blackpool at 14.10 hrs with the plan to display in Northern Ireland and then return to Exeter. It was known that one of the electrical generators was unserviceable, but with the display completed, the pilot noticed that the other generator had also failed. He climbed through cloud to FL220. With no radio, he elected to continue on his flight plan, descending to FL180 over North Wales to remain in visual flight conditions, slightly reducing power. Upon reaching his desired height, the pilot attempted to increase power, but found that the engine did not respond and would not relight. An attempt was made to glide to Llanbedr, but when the pilot realised that it could not be reached, he turned towards the nearest shoreline and ejected over an estuary. The aircraft fell in marshland and the pilot was injured on landing heavily in shallow water.

Hunter F.58A G-PSST, known as *Miss Demeanour*, is the most colourful Hunter to grace the skies. Originally built as RAF F.4 XF947 and delivered to 5 MU in 1956, this Hunter served with 3 Squadron at Geilenkirchen in RAF Germany. After a short career with the RAF, XF947 was allocated to the FAA at Arbroath as ground instruction airframe A2568. Having been bought back by Hawker in 1971, XF947 was converted to a F.58A for Switzerland and delivered in February 1972 as J-4104. It was allocated to target towing duties. When the Hunters were retired from Swiss service in 1996, J-4104 was ferried to Dunsfold and bought by Jonathan Whaley in 1997. After restoration by Jet Heritage at Hurn, the aircraft was painted in the startling scheme now carried. Since 1999, *Miss Demeanour* has been based at St Athan where she delights air show crowds.

Hunter trainers were popular with the Jet Set; mostly T.7s, like G-BOOM, were restored to fly. Hunter T.7 XL616 was first flown on 3 January 1959 and delivered to the RAF a month later. During its service it was converted to a T.7A, and in 1985 it was retired to No. 2 School of Technical Training (SofTT) at Cosford as instructional airframe 8837M. In 1993 it was moved to RAFC Cranwell as 9223M, and on 16 November 1993 it was withdrawn from use. On 17 October 1995 it was issued with a CofA as G-BWIE to Lansen Ltd at Bruntingthorpe, based at Cranfield. In July 1997, after flying at a number of air shows, it was transported by road to Kjula in Sweden, where it was registered SE-DXH on 9 January 1998. It was operated by Lansen from Bromma until the CofA expired in 2002, after which the aircraft was put into storage. It was put on static display in the Vaesteras Aircraft Museum in 2006.

Hunter T.7 XL578 joined Delta Jets at Kemble as a spares source and was never civil registered. Once all its useful parts had been removed, the hulk was dumped on its belly in the airfield fire training area. The airframe was rescued from fire practice and sent to Wickenby for restoration, and was then moved to a private owner at Kirkstead. Although reassembled, substantial parts were missing, such as the tailplane and nose cone. The aircraft was moved to Binbrook and then Cumbria, and was finally moved to the Laarbruch Museum for restoration and static display.

Hunter FGA.9 XF516/8885M at Farnborough, September 1998. (*Philip Birtles*)

Hunter FGA.9 XF516 no. 19 of 234 Squadron at Farnborough, July 2000. (*Philip Birtles*)

Hunter F.58 G-PSST at Kemble, June 2011. (*Philip Birtles*)

Hunter T.7 XL616 D at Cranfield, July 1996. (*Philip Birtles*)

Hunter T.7 XL578 at Kemble, July 2008. (*Philip Birtles*)

Like XL573, Hunter T.7 XL592 was acquired by Delta Jets for spares recovery and was not civil registered. It first flew on 30 August 1958 and was delivered to 229 OCU at Chivenor in September. When Chivenor closed in 1974, XL592 joined 1 TWU until retirement in 1984. This was followed by storage at St Athan. XL592 was issued to the Trade Management Training School at Scampton as 8836M. Following disposal, it was acquired by Delta Jets at Kemble, and upon their demise it was moved to Booker, next to Ockwells Manor near White Waltham airfield, in September 2014. At Booker it has been restored to static condition.

Hunter T.7 XL573 was bought by Barry Pover's Exeter-based Classic Jet Aircraft and registered G-BVGH. It was present statically at Farnborough in 1998 and Fairford in 2006. XL573 was grounded by 2007 and moved through a number of owners. In March 2011 the aircraft was with Hunter Flying at Exeter with the plan to display it for the Hunter's sixtieth anniversary show at Kemble in 2011. Unfortunately the restoration was not completed in time, but XL573 did fly later in the year and was in the static display at Fairford in July 2013, following which it was painted in an overall silver scheme. It was grounded in August 2015 and is now a static exhibit in the South Wales Aviation Museum at St Athan.

Hunter T.7 WV318 G-FFOX is painted in the smart all-black gloss of the Black Arrows. Built as an F.4, WV318 was delivered to 5 MU at Kemble on 16 June 1955, and served with 14 and 93 Squadrons. Following an accident in March 1956, the aircraft was returned to Hawker for repair, and at the same time was converted to a T.7. On return to the RAF on 1 June 1959, the aircraft was issued to the 111 Squadron 'Black Arrows'. WV318 then served with the CFS before

Hunter T.7 XL592 at Kemble, July 2008. (*Philip Birtles*)

Hunter T.7 XL573 at Fairford, July 2006. (*Philip Birtles*)

conversion to a T.7A. As a trainer, it flew with both 74 and 5 Squadrons, both equipped with Lightnings. It transferred to Buccaneer support duties with 12 Squadron in February 1970, moving through 15 and 16 Squadrons, before ending up with 208 Squadron at Lossiemouth. WV318 was one of four Hunter T.7s at Lossiemouth to be painted overall matt black to commemorate forty years of RAF Hunter service. These aircraft were among the last Hunters in regular service. Delta Jets bought WV318 in 1996 and registered her G-FFOX. The aircraft was flying again after a complete restoration on 2 May of that year. WV318 was a regular performer with Delta Jets. Upon their demise, it ended up based at Cranfield. It was grounded in August 2015 following the accident at Shoreham.

Probably the most attractive colour scheme of any Hunter was that given to T.7 XL577 (G-XMHD and G-BXKF) when it was restored by Delta Jets and painted in the 92 Squadron 'Blue Diamonds' colours of XL571. XL577 made its first post-restoration flight from Kemble in December 2004 and was a popular air show performer until Delta Jets ceased trading in 2011. The aircraft was then stored outside, but fortunately Midair Squadron rescued it and flew it again in May 2014, replacing the colours with an overall silver scheme to match their Canberra PR.9. Midair was liquidated in 2015 when all civil Hunters were grounded. XL577 was bought by a Jordanian owner and departed for Jordan on 2 May 2016.

Hunter T.7 XL600 first flew on 7 October 1958 and was delivered to 65 Squadron the following month. Later it moved to the Wattisham Station Flight, then 4 FTS at Valley, and finally 16 Squadron. It was acquired as a civilian aircraft,

Hunter T.8 WV318, painted as of 111 Squadron, at Kemble, June 2010. (*Philip Birtles*)

Hunter T.7 XL577/G-BXKF, painted as V of 92 Squadron, at Fairford, July 2008. (*Philip Birtles*)

Hunter T.7 XL577/G-XMHD at Fairford, July 2014. (*Philip Birtles*)

registered G-VETA at Hurn, and participated in the fighter meet at North Weald in 1996. It was then sold to Gordon Hannam who based it with Delta Jets at Kemble until 2004, when it was sold to Gower Jets and based at North Weald and Cranwell. Following a brief time with Team Viper at Kemble, G-VETA was bought by Midair Squadron in August 2013 and painted in the overall silver scheme. In 2014 the Hunter was grounded for a major inspection, but Midair ceased to operate in 2015 before the maintenance was completed. XL600 was put up for auction and Canada's Jet Aircraft Museum in Ontario made the successful bid. It was delivered to London, Ontario, on 28 May 2016, with plans to restore it to flying.

A pair of Hunter T.8Cs were delivered to Exeter in 1995, but neither achieved much flying. Hunter T.8 WT722 was originally built as an F.4 and first flown on 4 February 1955. Following delivery to the RAF, it served with 54 and 26 Squadrons. Hawker bought WT722 back in 1957 for conversion to one of the early T.8s, with delivery to the FAA on 10 April 1959. The aircraft served with 703 and 764 NAS at Lossiemouth, and 759 NAS at Brawdy. In 1970 the aircraft was transferred to the Air Director School (ADS) at Yeovilton, which was later merged into FRADU in 1972. By 1983, WT722 was the oldest Hunter flying. It was retired in 1994 to Shawbury with 9,500 flying hours recorded and 12,500 landings. It was sold to Classic Jet Aircraft at Exeter in 1995 to become G-BWGN, but the CofA expired in 1997 and the aircraft was moved to Delta Jets at Kemble in 2006 as a static aircraft. In May 2010, WT722 was moved to Airbase at Coventry, and then to the new facility at St Mawgan in 2012, where it is now based. The other T.8C was XE665, which served with 118 Squadron as an F.4 in RAF Germany before being converted by Hawker. XE665 was delivered to 764 NAS and then transferred to the Yeovilton Station Flight and painted in the colours of an admiral's barge. XE665 then went on to operate with 759 and 738 NAS at Brawdy, with a return to Yeovilton with the ADS and FRADU. It spent some time with 237 OCU at Honington, before finishing its career with FRADU again at Yeovilton. When it was registered to the Hunter Flying Club at Exeter as G-BWGM, the intention was to return the aircraft to admiral's barge colours, but the sponsorship required was not achieved. A move was made to Delta Jets at Kemble as part of the static line-up on the airfield, and with the collapse of Delta, Midair took it over and painted it in overall silver with RAF markings, including a tail flash for use as a static aircraft. With the collapse of Midair in 2015, XE665 was held in open storage on the airfield before being put on static display, together with a Gnat.

Hunter T.7 WV372 was delivered to the RAF in July 1955 as an F.4. It was damaged by fire and returned to Hawker for repair and conversion to a T.7. It returned to service in 1959 and was operated by 2 Squadron in RAF Germany among other units. It was retired from the RAF in 1998 and registered G-BXFI, based at North Weald, although it was often on the flight lines at Kemble and Fairford. On 22 August 2015, WV372 was scheduled to display at Shoreham, but crashed at the start of its programme when it failed to complete a loop, hitting the

Hunter T.7 XL600 no. 83 of 4 FTS at Biggin Hill, September 1974. (*Philip Birtles*)

Hunter T.7 G-VETA/XL600 at Kemble, June 2009. (*Philip Birtles*)

Hunter T.8C WT722 of 878 FRADU/G-BWGN at Kemble, June 2009. (*Philip Birtles*)

Hunter T.8C XE665 of 876 FRADU/G-BWGM at Kemble, June 2009. (*Philip Birtles*)

A27 outside the airfield boundary, killing eleven people. The pilot was critically injured, but survived. As a result of this accident, all civil-registered Hunters were grounded pending the accident investigation, and restrictions were placed on all other air shows in Britain. The official investigation concluded that the crash was caused by pilot error, and therefore there was no inherent fault with the aircraft. On 24 August 2015, in addition to the grounding of civilian Hunters, the CAA imposed restrictions on all vintage jets performing over land-based air shows until further notice. In January 2016 the CAA brought in even stricter conditions for air shows in the UK, but on 6 July 2017 the grounding of Hunters was lifted, although they were subject to enhanced inspections and maintenance. Although the ban on straight-wing military jet aircraft performing manoeuvres in public was lifted in March 2018, the ban remains on swept-wing aircraft.

Still remaining in the UK as a potential flyer is Hunter T.8C WV322, which was built as an F.4 and first flown on 8 June 1955. It was delivered to the RAF on 28 June and served with 43 and 92 Squadrons before returning to Hawker for conversion to a T.8C. When it was delivered to the FAA it served with 764 NAS, followed by 809 NAS for Buccaneer training. When Buccaneers were retired from the FAA, WV322 rejoined the RAF with 237 OCU at Honington and was still used for Buccaneer training. On retirement from flying, WV322 was allocated to Cranwell for technical training until it was put up for disposal in early 2001. The aircraft was bought by Chris Perkins and registered G-BZSE. It was flown to Kemble on 14 February to be prepared for full permit-to-fly status by Delta Jets,

Hunter T.7 WV372, painted as R of 2 Squadron, at Kemble, June 2011. (*Philip Birtles*)

and returned to the air again on 13 March 2002. After a few changes of ownership, WV322 is now based at North Weald, looking smart in admiral's barge livery, and may soon become one of the few Hunters left to be seen in British skies.

On the face of it, Hunter T.8C N-321 looks very Dutch, but it did not see military service in the Netherlands. It was built as F.4 XF357 and served with 130 Squadron RAF. It was returned to Hawker for conversion to a T.8 and delivered to the FAA at Lossiemouth. Following a range of duties, it was finally with FRADU at Yeovilton until retirement in 1994. XF357 was then delivered to Jet Heritage at Hurn for restoration as G-BWGL for a private owner. With the demise of Jet Heritage it was acquired by the Old Flying Machine Company. Restoration was completed by Classic Jet Aircraft, and XF357 was painted in the colours of the T.7 prototype XJ615. During the restoration, the Harley light was removed but the arrester hook was retained. In mid-May 2007, XF357 was bought by the Dutch Hawker Hunter Foundation based at Leeuwarden. Dutch two-seat Hunters carried the serials N-301 to N-320, and permission was given by the Dutch Air Force for this aircraft to adopt the identity N-321. The aircraft made a rare visit to Kemble in June 2011.

Hunter F.58 J-4025 was first flown on 23 February 1959 and delivered to Switzerland on 23 March. It was allocated to 20 Staffel on 27 April, where it served until it was allocated to the Patrouille Suisse in June 1981. It was withdrawn from use on 16 December 1994 and presented to the RAF Benevolent Fund in Jordanian colours as 712 on 22 July 1995, flying to Hurn on 12 October as G-BWKG. On 29 September 1999 it was delivered to the Royal Jordanian Historic Flight in Amman, but by 2009 it was grounded.

Delta Jets at Kemble was certainly a great place to see Hunters, but only a few were able to fly, many being held in reserve as a source of spares. At least it was a source of Hunters for UK aviation museums, although there is no shortage of preserved Hunters in Britain.

Although all civil-registered Hunters were grounded in September 2015, aircraft on the military register were allowed to continue flying. Hawker Hunter Aviation, based at RAF Scampton, was started by Mat Potulski when, in the early 1990s, he joined with Mark Hanna to investigate the potential of operating outsourced military training, similar to aggressor training in the USA. A fast low-cost jet fleet needed to be created, and although a number of types were considered, the retirement of the Swiss Hunters provided the ideal answer. The aircraft were often low hours and had been well maintained with affordable operating costs; a fleet of twelve single-seat F.58s were bought and hangared at Scampton. Sadly Mark Hanna was killed in a vintage aircraft crash, which delayed the start of the project, but by 1999 Potulski had made the decision to create Hawker Hunter Aviation (HHA), which was formed in 2000 with fourteen Hunters, including a trio of two-seat aircraft, as well as a collection ex-military combat aircraft which could be returned to flight if a suitable contract was awarded. The two-seat aircraft were T.8C XF994 (registered G-CGHU), T.8B XF995 (used by the ETPS at Boscombe Down and registered G-BZSE), and T.7 XL587 (registered G-HPUX). The

Hunter T.8 WV322 at North Weald, September 2019. (*Philip Birtles*)

Dutch Hunter N-321 at Kemble, June 2011. (*Philip Birtles*)

Hunter F.58 Jordanian 712 E/G-BWKC at Farnborough. (*Philip Birtles*)

company employed eight ex-RAF maintenance engineers and succeeded in gaining AvP67 status, which was the approval needed to confirm HHA's maintenance and operating standards. These standards are equivalent to military levels, and AvP67 status allowed the company to bid for MOD contracts. The flying, meanwhile, was, and still is, done by a group of retained former military pilots. The initial contract was placed in 2007 when two HHA Hunters in full military markings started a series of trials with FRA, using the Hunters as targets for the new Sampson radars fitted to the Royal Navy new Type 45 destroyers. This was the first time such a task had been outsourced to a private fast jet contractor. The Hunters, which operated from Bournemouth, provided fast agile targets and were ideal in offering viceless handling, good subsonic performance, excellent reliability and good internal and external payload.

These Hunters are fitted with radar warning receivers (RWR), chaff/flare dispensers, and are capable of carrying the latest ACMI and electronic warfare (EW) pods. The aircraft are usually configured with up to four underwing fuel tanks or EW pods, with the fuel capacity allowing up to two and a half hours' endurance. Hunters ZZ190 and ZZ191 are usually based at Yeovilton, operating under MOD contract and providing a realistic training capability for the Royal Navy. ZZ190 first flew on 22 August 1959 as J-4066 and was delivered to Emmen on 25 September, joining the Swiss Air Force on 7 October. It was modified to carry AIM-9 Sidewinders air-to-air missiles and Maverick air-to-ground weapons. J-4066 was retired on 6 December 1994 and flown to Caen for preservation on 13 July 1995. Ray and Mark Hanna bought the aircraft and it was ferried to Delta Jets at Kemble for maintenance, becoming G-BXNZ. It was delivered to

Hunter T.8 XF995 HHA at Greenham Common, May 1980. (*Philip Birtles*)

Hunter T.7 XL587 TWU at Greenham Common, July 1976. (*Philip Birtles*)

HHA at Scampton in June 1999 and registered G-HHAE on 10 December 2002. The civil registration was replaced by military markings ZZ190 on 2 January 2007. Hunter F.58 first flew as J-4058 on 25 June 1959 and was delivered to Emmen on 14 August. It served with 2 and 15 Staffel and was armed with AIM-9 Sidewinders and AGM-58 Mavericks. J-4058 was retired from Swiss service on 24 November 1994 at Meiringen and flown to Southend on 28 June 1995. It went to Exeter for maintenance on 14 July 1995 as G-BWFS, and then The Old Flying Machine Company (OFMC) at Duxford on 24 July 1995. It was flown to HHA at Scampton on 10 December 2002 as G-HHAD, and was re-registered ZZ191 on 8 November 2006. Both Hunters operate under civil-owned military aircraft (COMA) regulations on defence simulation and systems trials.

A recent addition to the HHA fleet in September 2018 was Hunter T72 PP-XHH from Embraer in Brazil. The aircraft had been built as F.4 XE704 in 1955. In July 1963, when it was replaced by F.6s, it was retired to Halton as 7788M. It was bought back by Hawker and converted as T.66 J-736 in 1974 for the Chilean Air Force. HHA overhauled the aircraft; it had engine runs at Scampton in November 2019 and took its first flight as XE688 on 29 January 2020.

In Canada, Northern Light have operated a fleet of twelve ex-Swiss Hunter F.58s on aggressor training since 2002. Unlike at HHA, the Canadian Hunters are on the civil register. They are flown by experienced fighter pilots. The company have contracts with Canadian, US and other NATO air, ground and naval forces, providing training in electronic warfare, target-towing, air-to-air gunnery, aggressor fighters, attack simulations, air intercept and forward air controller training. The Hunters are more cost-effective and fly further, faster, higher and longer than most other aggressor types available. These Hunters feature ACMI, threat emitters, jammers, chaff/flare dispensers, radar warning receivers and have

Ex-Swiss Air Force Hunter F.58 J-4031 at Duxford in June 1997 as part of the HHA stock. (*Philip Birtles*)

Hunter F.58A ZZ190 HHA at Fairford, July 2019. (*Philip Birtles*)

Ex-Swiss Hunter F.58 J-4058/G-HHAD at Waddington, June 2003. This aircraft later became ZZ191. (*Philip Birtles*)

Hunter F.58A ZZ191 HHA at Fairford, July 2019. (*Philip Birtles*)

Ex-Chilean two-seat Hunter PP-XHH used by Embraer in Brazil as a flight test chase aircraft, and bought by HHA at Scampton. (*BAE Systems*)

a typical endurance of up to three hours. In more advanced air combat training, Northern Light can provide two *v.* two aircraft, four *v.* four, and more. In major international exercises such as Red Flag, Maple Flag or fighter weapons instructor courses, the Hunters can add training quality to the designated opposing forces.

In addition to UK-based flying Hunters, there are some flying in Switzerland and New Zealand. Examples are F.58 ZU-AVG, painted in tiger markings, and ex-Singapore Air Force JIL517 flying in New Zealand.

Canadian Northern Light military facilities Hunter F.58 C-GIMP. (*BAE Systems*)

ATAC-operated Hunter F.58 N330AX. (*BAE Systems*)

Swiss-operated Hunter F.58 ZU-AVG in startling tiger markings. (*BAE Systems*)

Ex-Singapore Air Force Hunter F.74 JIL517, flying in New Zealand. (*BAE Systems*)

APPENDIX I

Hunter Survivors, UK

With hundreds of Hunters surviving around the world, including a reported fourteen FGA.9s in Zimbabwe and two in Lebanon as unlikely flyers, plus ex-Singapore Hunters in Australia and New Zealand, it is impossible to maintain an up-to-date record of survivors and their condition worldwide. There are more Hunters surviving in Asia, the Indian sub-continent, North America, South America, Africa and Europe, making it probably numerically the most preserved aircraft type globally. The aim of this appendix is to record as accurately as possible Hunter survivors in the UK, with illustrations where possible.

Mark	Serial	Location	Remarks
F.1	WT555	Vanguard Holdings, Greenford, London	First production aircraft ex-7499M Locking Nov. '57 & Cosford
F.1	WT569	2117 Sqn ATC, Kenfig Hill, Mid Glamorgan, Wales	A&AEE 7.54, 7491M at St Athan Nov. '57
F.1	WT612	Gate guard, RAF Henlow, May 1984	Avon development, Yatesbury as 7496M, Hereford Sept. '63, Halton Jan. '83
F.1	WT619	Cosford, ex-Manchester Museum of Science & Industry	43 Sqn, 222 Sqn, 233 OCU, 7525M St Athan, Henlow
F.1	WT651	Newark Air Museum, Jan. '92, 222 Sqn colours	222 Sqn, 229 OCU, 233 OCU, Weeton 7532M Nov. '57
F.1	WT660	Highland Aircraft Preservation Society, Inverness Airport, closed 2019. C:43 Sqn	DFLS, 229 OCU Carlisle 14 MU gate as 7421M Apr. '57
F.1	WT680	Anglia Motel, Fleet Hargate, 2430 ATC Sqn	DFLS, 7533M Weeton Jan. '57, Aberporth
F.1	WT694	Caernarfon Air World, Gwynedd, Wales, Sept. '95, 245 Sqn markings	54 Sqn, DFLS, 229 OCU, Debden 7510M Nov. '57, Newton

F.1 WT555 at RAF Museum Cosford, October 1979. (*Philip Birtles*)

F.1 WT612 at RAF Henlow, May 2014. (*Philip Birtles*)

F.1 WT651 at Newark Air Museum, November 2015. (*Philip Birtles*)

F.1 WT660 at 14 MU gate in Carlisle, July 1970. (*Philip Birtles*)

F.1 WT680 at Aberporth as Z:DFLS, July 1980. (*Philip Birtles*)

F.1 WT694 on Debden gate as Y:DFLS, May 1969. (*Philip Birtles*)

F.2	WN904	Sywell Aviation Museum, Sywell, Northants, Aug. '12	257 Sqn, 7544M Halton, Melksham, Newton, Duxford, Waterbeach
F.3	WB188	Tangmere Military Aviation Museum, West Sussex, Sept. '92	Prototype 7154M Halton Nov. '54, Melksham, Colerne, St Athan, Cosford
F.4	WT746	Dumfries & Galloway Aviation Museum 1999, 43 Sqn colours	AFDS, 7770M Halton Nov. '62, Saighton
F.5	WP185	Paul & Andy Wood, Great Dunmow, stored	1 Sqn, 34 Sqn, Henlow, as 7583M Oct. '58, Hendon, Abingdon
F.5	WP190	Tangmere Military Aviation Museum, June '02	1 Sqn, Bircham Newton as 7582M Sept. '58, Finningley, Upwood, Stanbridge as 8473M, Hucclecote, Quedgeley

F.2 WN904 at Duxford, June 1974. (*Philip Birtles*)

Opposite above: F.2 WN904 of 1 Squadron at Waterbeach, June 1996. (*Philip Birtles*)

Opposite below: F.3 WB188 at Melksham gate, August 1967. (*Philip Birtles*)

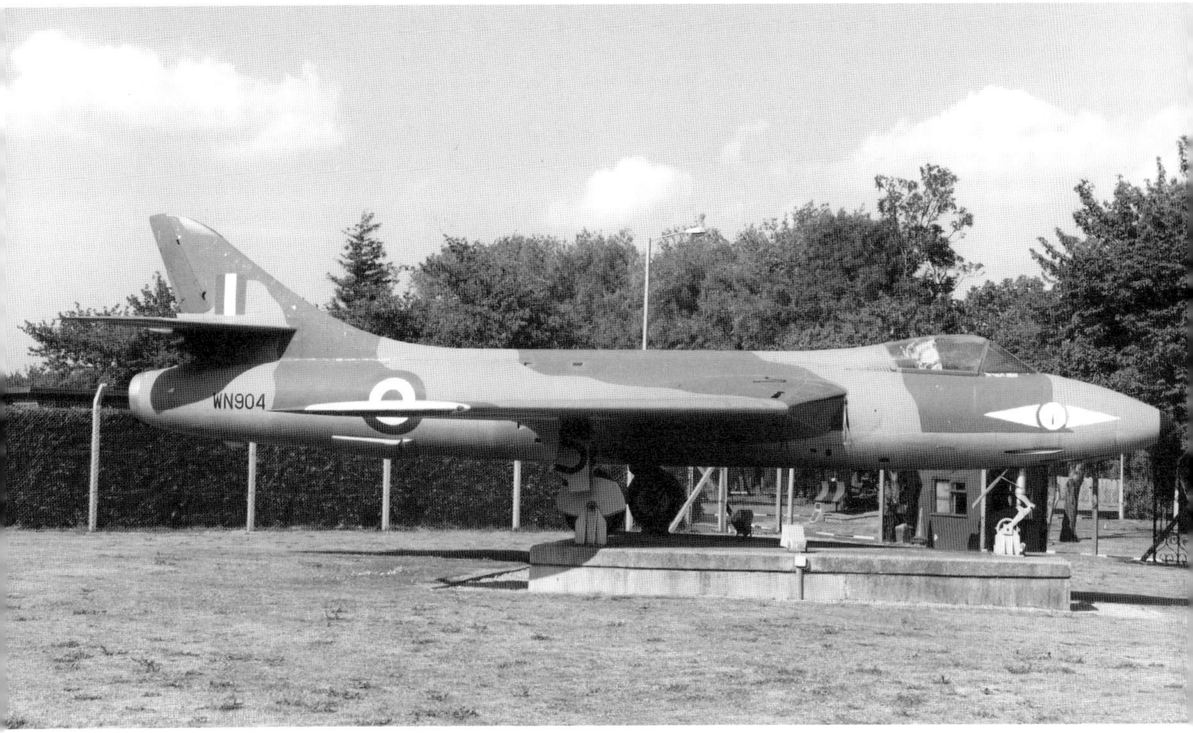
WN904

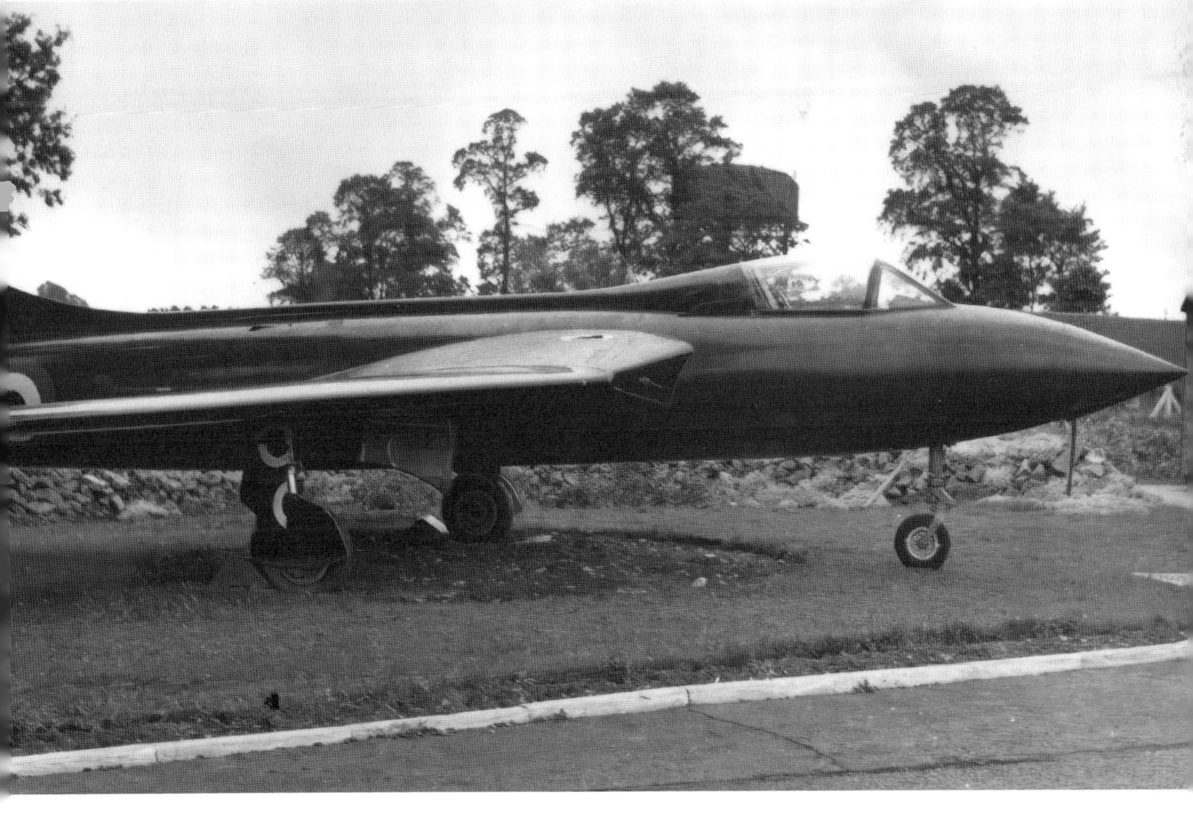

F.3 WB188 at Colerne Museum, July 1975. (*Philip Birtles*)

F.3 WB188 IAT at Greenham Common, July 1976. (*Philip Birtles*)

F.5 WP185 at Henlow, May 1969. (*Philip Birtles*)

F.6	XF375	Boscombe Down Aviation Collection, Old Sarum, Apr. '07, ETPS markings	R-R, EE, ETPS, Cranwell as 8736M Jan. '82, Boscombe Down
F.6	XF509	Fort Paull, closed late 2019	54 Sqn, AFDS, 4 FTS Thurleigh, Chivenor, as 8708M Dec. '81
F.6	XF526	Graham Revill, Birlingham, Worcester	66 Sqn, 63 Sqn, 56 Sqn, 43 Sqn, 56 Sqn, 229 OCU, 4 FTS to 8679M Halton Nov. '81, St Athan
F.6	XF527	RAF Halton parade ground	19 Sqn, CFE, 4 FTS, to Halton as 8680M Apr. '81
F.6	XG160	Bournemouth Aviation Museum, Hurn	43 Sqn, 111 Sqn, 229 OCU, 1 TWU to 8831M at Scampton, ex-Jet Heritage
F.6	XG164	Davidstow Moor, 111 Sqn colours, July '14	111 Sqn, 74 Sqn, to 8681M Halton Apr. '81, Shawbury
F.6	XG210	Beck Row, Mildenhall, private collection	14 Sqn, 19 Sqn, CFE, Cranfield, Hatfield, DRA Bedford soc Sept. '85
F.6	XG274	Privately owned, Newmarket	14 Sqn, 66 Sqn, 229 OCU, 4 FTS, to Halton as 8710M Nov. '81
F.6	XJ690	Bournemouth Aviation Museum gate	14 Sqn, to FGA.9 Oct. '64, 20 Sqn, HSA Feb. '76, nose fitted to ET-273

F.6 XF375 at Greenham Common, July 1976. (*Philip Birtles*)

F.6 XF509 at Cottesmore, July 1971. (*Philip Birtles*)

F.6 XF527 on gate at Halton, March 1987. (*Philip Birtles*)

F.6 XG210 at Cranfield, June 1966. (*Philip Birtles*)

F.6 XG210 at Hatfield, July 1974. (*Philip Birtles*)

F.6 XG274 at Gaydon as 71 4FTS, September 1996. (*Philip Birtles*)

F.6A	XE606	8 Squadron Waddington, static display as 'XE620' Apr. '13. The real XE620 was sold to India	CFE, 54 Sqn, 65 Sqn, 74 Sqn, 92 Sqn, 229 OCU, TWU, to 8841M Laabruch, Cottesmore
F.6A	XE627	IWM Duxford T:65 Sqn, May '73	65 Sqn, 92 Sqn, 229 OCU, 54 Sqn, 1 Sqn, TWU
F.6A	XF382	Midland Air Museum, Coventry, Dec. '86. 15 234 Sqn markings	AWA built, 92 Sqn, 63 Sqn, 65 Sqn, FCS, 229 OCU, TWU
F.6A	XG172	City of Norwich Aviation Museum, Feb. '01, marked as XG168 79 Sqn	19 Sqn, 263 Sqn, 229 OCU, 1 TWU, to Scampton as 8832M Sept. '84
F.6A	XG225	RAF Museum Cosford gate 1988, 237 OCU markings	20 Sqn, 74 Sqn, 92 Sqn, 229 OCU, 2 SofTT as 8713M Feb. '82

F.6A XE606 with 4 Squadron, Cottesmore, July 2000. (*Philip Birtles*)

F.6A XE606 with 8 Squadron at Waddington, July 2014. (*Philip Birtles*)

F.6A XE627 at IWM Duxford, May 2006. (*Philip Birtles*)

F.6A XF382 at Midland Air Museum, Baginton, May 2010. (*Philip Birtles*)

F.6A XG172 of 229 OCU and 63 Squadron at Wattisham, August 1967. (*Philip Birtles*)

F.6A XG225 on the gate at RAF Museum Cosford. (*Philip Birtles*)

T.7	WV383	FAST Farnborough Apr. '00	RAFFC as F.4, Gutersloh, Jever, 28 Sqn, RAE, DERA
T.7	XL563	FAST Farnborough Apr. '14	IAM, RAE Farnborough, Hereford as 9218M June '95
T.7	XL565	Bruntingthorpe Mar. '02	8 Sqn, 1417 Flt, 208 Sqn, 4 FTS, 237 OCU, FRADU, soc Oct. '93
T.7	XL569	Aeropark, East Midlands Airport Feb. '93	229 OCU, TWU, 12 Sqn, 237 OCU, 15 Sqn, to Cosford as 8833M Sept. '84
T.7	XL572	Yorkshire Air Museum, Elvington, Jan. '95. Marked as XL571 92 Sqn 'Blue Diamonds'	229 OCU, TWU, to Cosford as 8834M Aug. '84 G-HNTR
T.7	XL573	South Wales Aviation Museum, St Athan as G-BVGH, Dec. '11	FCS, 229 OCU, 4 FTS, 237 OCU
T.7	XL586	Action Park, North Benfleet	229 OCU, TWU, BAe Warton, Shawbury, Kemble
T.7	XL591	Gatwick Aviation Museum, Charlwood, 2002, 4 FTS colours	FCS, 229 OCU, 4 FTS, RAE, 237 OCU, 208 Sqn, Kemble soc Oct. '93
T.7	XL612	Swansea Airport, 8 Jan. '12, in ETPS colours	402 WTS, 43 Sqn, ETPS final flight 10 Aug. '01, stored at Exeter
T.7	XL618	Unknown, ex-Newark Air Museum, ex-Carernarfon Air Museum, to Newark May '14	Gutersloh Stn Flt, Jever Stn Flt, 229 OCU
T.7	XL621	Privately owned, Dunsfold ex G-BNCX, ETPS colours	Gutersloh & Jever Stn Flts, 4 FTS, ETPS, Brooklands
T.7	XL623	Hawker Association, Dunsfold, July '18. Last Kingston-built Hunter	65 Sqn, 208 Sqn, 92 Sqn, 43 Sqn, 1 Sqn, 19 Sqn, 74 Sqn, 1 TWU, to Cosford as 8770M Dec. '82
T.7	XM121	Alba Power, Netherley, Aberdeen ex-Dutch N-315	Amsterdam NLS spares, Batley, Hucclecote, Long Marston
T.7	XX467	Newark Air Museum, ex-XL605/G-TVII May '17	92 Sqn, 66 Sqn, Saudi 70-617, Jordan 836, XX467 TWU, soc Oct. '83, Kemble, Exeter, Bruntingthorpe
T.7A	XL568	RAF Museum, Cosford Feb. '02 in 74 Sqn colours	74 Sqn, 237 OCU, 208 Sqn, 12 Sqn, to Cranwell as 9224M Nov. '93

T.7 WV383 FAST at Farnborough, November 2008. (*Philip Birtles*)

T.7 XL563 at Abingdon, September 1971. (*Philip Birtles*)

T.7 XL565 at Bruntingthorpe, June 2017. (*Philip Birtles*)

T.7 XL569 at Chivenor, August 1969. (*Philip Birtles*)

T.7 XL572 at Yorkshire Air Museum, Elvington, in 92 Squadron colours, July 2000. (*Philip Birtles*)

T.7 XL573 at Farnborough, September 1998. (*Philip Birtles*)

T.7 XL591 at Finningley, July 1977. (*Philip Birtles*)

T.7 XL612 at Swansea Airport, June 2017. (*Philip Birtles*)

T.7 XL618 at Newark Air Museum, November 2015. (*Philip Birtles*)

T.7 XL623 at Chivenor, August 1969. (*Philip Birtles*)

T.7 XM121/N-315 at Long Marston, August 1996. (*Philip Birtles*)

T.7 XX467 at Newark Air Museum, May 2019. (*Philip Birtles*)

T.7A XL568 at RAF Museum Cosford in 111 Squadron fortieth-anniversary markings, May 2002. (*Philip Birtles*)

T.8C	WT722	Cornwall Aviation Heritage Centre, July '12	54 Sqn, 26 Sqn, to T.8 703 NAS, 764 NAS, FRADU, Shawbury, Exeter, Kemble, Coventry
T.8C	WT799	Blue Lagoon Diving Centre, Womersley. Probably now submerged in a lake for scuba training	F.4 111 Sqn, 4 Sqn T.8 Feb. '59, 764 NAS, 759 NAS, FRADU, last flew Sept. '82, Shawbury, North Weald
T.8C	WV396	RAF Valley gate on a pole in 4 FTS colours '97 as 9249M, now replaced by a Hawk	20 Sqn, 26 Sqn, 229 OCU, to T.8, 759 NAS, ADS Yeovilton, wfu 1986, Shawbury
T.8M	XL580	FAA Museum, Yeovilton, 899 NAS colours	764 NAS, FRADU as T.8C
T.8M	XL602	Global Air Services, St Athan as G-BWFT	764 NAS, 759 NAS, FRADU, Shawbury, Exeter

T.8 WT722 at FRADU, Yeovilton, September 1970. (*Philip Birtles*)

T.8C WT722 at Cornwall Aviation Heritage Centre, St Mawgan, October 2013. (*Philip Birtles*)

T.8C WV396 at RAF Valley gate, August 2001. (*Philip Birtles*)

T.8 XL580 at FRADU, Yeovilton, September 1970. (*Philip Birtles*)

T.8M XL580 at the FAA Museum, Yeovilton, September 2013, in 899 NAS markings. (*Philip Birtles*)

FGA.9	XE624	Wickenby Aerodrome, Lincs	1 Sqn, 229 OCU, TWU, to Brawdy as 8875M, Oct. '85
FGA.9	XG154	RAF Museum, Hendon, May '85, 8/43 Sqn colours	54 Sqn, 43 Sqn, 229 OCU TWU, to St Athan as 8863M
FGA.9	XG194	Wattisham Heritage Centre, Nov. '09. 111 Sqn colours No. 1 Black Arrows—Roger Topp	43 Sqn, 111 Sqn, FGA.9, 1 Sqn, TWU, to Cosford as 8839M Oct. '84, North Luffenham
FGA.9	XG254	Norfolk & Suffolk Museum, Flixton, Feb. '02, 54 Sqn colours	54 Sqn, 229 OCU, TWU, St Athan, to Coltishall as 8881M, Dec. '85

FGA.9 XE624 as G1 TWU at Leuchars, September 1981. (*Philip Birtles*)

FGA.9 XG154 at RAF Museum Hendon. (*Philip Birtles*)

FGA.9 XG194 of 79 Squadron at Coltishall, September 1974. (*Philip Birtles*)

FR.10	XF426	RAF Museum, Hendon Oman Air Force colours, 2003	F.6 del '56, 208 Sqn, FR.10, Jordan as 853, Oman
FR.10	XJ714	East Midlands Aeropark, May '09	Long Marston, composite of many different Hunter parts

GA.11	WT711	Lakes Lightnings, Spark Bridge, Cumbria	14 Sqn to GA.11, 738 NAS, 764 NAS, FRU, FRADU, to A2731 at Shawbury, Sept. '85, to A2645 at Culdrose, Coventry
GA.11	WT806	Classic British Jets, Bruntingthorpe	14 Sqn, CFS, to GA.11, FRADU
GA.11	WV256	Cornwall Aviation Heritage Centre, July '12, in 26 Squadron colours	26 Sqn, 229 OCU, to GA.11, 738 NAS, FRADU
GA.11	WV382	East Midlands Aeropark, Jan. '09	67 Sqn, to GA.11, 738 NAS, FRU, FRADU, to A2730 at Lee-on-Solent, Long Marston
GA.11	WW654	Gate guard at former RNAS Ford	98 Sqn, 4 Sqn, 229 OCU, to GA.11, 738 NAS, FRADU, to Culdrose as A2753, Feb. '87
GA.11	XE668	Hambuger Hill Paintball, Marksbury, Somerset	4 Sqn, 26 Sqn, to GA.11, 738 NAS, FRADU, to Culdrose as A2733, Feb. '85, with SAH, Predannack as A2647

FR.10 XJ714 at Long Marston, August 1996. (*Philip Birtles*)

FR.10 XJ714 at East Midlands Aeropark, June 2017. (*Philip Birtles*)

GA.11 WT711 with 837 FRU at Yeovilton, September 1973. Note the Harley light. (*Philip Birtles*)

GA.11 WT711 in SAH markings at Coventry, August 2010. (*Philip Birtles*)

GA.11 WT806 as one of the 838 FRADU 'Blue Herons' at Greenham Common, June 1979. (*Philip Birtles*)

GA.11 WT806 at Bruntingthorpe, June 2017. (*Philip Birtles*)

GA.11 WV256 with 732 VL FRU at Yeovilton, September 1973. (*Philip Birtles*)

GA.11 WV256 as 'WB188' at Cornwall Aviation Heritage Centre, St Mawgan, October 2013. (*Philip Birtles*)

GA.11 WV382 at East Midlands Aeropark, June 2017. (*Philip Birtles*)

Danish F.51s in the UK:

F.51	E-409	City of Norwich Aviation Museum in 74 Squadron colours as 'XE683', Oct. '95	Esk 724, Dunsfold as G-9-437, Dec. '75, Cardiff
F.51	E-412	Brooklands Museum fuselage marked as 'XF368 4 Sq', Sept. '05	Esk 724, Dunsfold as G-9-439, Mar. '76, Wycombe Air Park
F.51	E-419	NE Aircraft Museum, Sunderland, July '77	Esk 724, Dunsfold as G-9-441
F.51	E-421	Brooklands Museum, Mar. '89	Esk 724, Dunsfold as G-9-443, May '76, Brooklands Tech
F.51	E-425	Solway Aviation Museum, Carlisle in ETPS colours as 'XG190', Nov. '08	Esk 724, Dunsfold as G-9-446, Coventry
F.51	E-428	South Yorks Aircraft Museum, Doncaster marked as 'WV314', 1988	Esk 724, Dunsfold as G-9-445 Feb. '76, East Kirkby, Firbeck
F.51	E-430	Gatwick Aviation Museum, Charlwood, in FAA colours as 'XF418'	Esk 724, Dunsfold as G-9-448

F.51 E-409 at Cardiff, August 1980. (*Philip Birtles*)

F.51 E-412, painted as XF384 of 4 Squadron, at Brooklands Museum, June 2018. (*Philip Birtles*)

F.51 E-421 at Brooklands Museum, Weybridge, January 2009. (*Philip Birtles*)

F.51 ex-Danish E-425 Esk 724 at Coventry, May 1995. (*Philip Birtles*)

F.51 E-425 'XG190' at Solway Aviation Museum, September 2014. (*Philip Birtles*)

Some Hunters grounded by RAF and restored to fly again for export:

F.4	WV266	To Halton as 7781M, seen Sept. '70	To HAL July '72, converted to F.58A J-4146, to Switzerland Oct. '74
F.4	WV272	To Halton as 7892M, seen Sept. '70	To HAL 9.71, converted to T.75A 540, to Singapore July '73
F.4	WV398	Gate guard at Spitalgate, seen June '68	To HAL and converted to T.68 J-4203, to Switzerland Mar. '75
F.4	WW653	To Halton as 7784M, seen Sept. '70	To HAL Jan. '72, converted to FGA.71 J-737, to Chile Jan. '74
F.4	XF365	At Lee-on-Solent, seen June '68, painted as GA.11, but with gun pack	To HSA Aug. '69, converted to F.58A J-4109, to Switzerland May '72
F.4	XF369	To Halton as 7914M, seen June '68	To HSA Feb. '71, converted to FR.24B 538, to Singapore Apr. '73
F.4	XF946	To Bicester as 7804M, seen Apr. '68 and used as travelling exhibit	To Jordanian War Memorial, Amman as static aircraft

F.4 WV266 at Halton, September 1970. (*Philip Birtles*)

F.4 WV272 at Halton, September 1970. (*Philip Birtles*)

F.4 WV398 at Spitalgate, June 1968. (*Philip Birtles*)

F.4 WW653 at Halton, September 1970. (*Philip Birtles*)

F.4 XF365 at Lee-on-Solent, June 1968. (*Philip Birtles*)

F.4 XF369 at Halton, June 1968. (*Philip Birtles*)

F.4 XF946 at Bicester, April 1968. (*Philip Birtles*)

APPENDIX II

Hunter Production

Mark	Number in Batch	Factory	Serial Numbers
F.1	First batch of 113	Kingston	WT555–595, WT611–660, WT679–700
F.1	Second batch of 26	Blackpool	WW599–610, WW632–645
F.2	One batch of 45	Coventry	WN888–921, WN943–953
F.4	First batch of 85	Kingston	WT701–723, WT734–780, WT795–811
F.4	Second batch of 100	Kingston	WV253–281, WV324–412
F.4	Third batch of 3	Kingston	WW589–591
F.4	Fourth batch of 20	Blackpool	WW646–665
F.4	Fifth batch of 100	Blackpool	XE657–689, XE702–718, XF289–324, XF357–370
F.4	Sixth batch of 57	Blackpool	XF932–953, XF967–999, XG341–342
F.5	One batch of 105	Coventry	WN954–992, WP101–150, WP179–194
F.6	One prototype	Kingston	XF833
F.6	First batch of 7	Kingston	WW592–598
F.6	Second batch of 100	Kingston	XE526–561, XE579–628, XE643–656
F.6	Third batch of 110	Kingston	XG127–137, XG150–172, XG185–211, XG225–239, XG251–274, XG289–298
F.6	Fourth batch of 45	Kingston	XJ632–646, XJ673–695, XJ712–718
F.6	Fifth batch of 53	Kingston	XK136–224. XK157–224 to India
F.6	One batch of 100	Coventry	XF373–389, XF414–463, XF495–527
T.7	Two prototypes	Kingston	XJ615, XJ627
T.7	One batch of 45	Kingston	XL563–583, XL586–587, XL591 597, XL600–601, XL605, XL609–623
T.8	One prototype	Kingston	WW664
T.8	One batch of 10	Kingston	XL580–582, XL584–585, XL598–599, XL602–604
F.4	One batch of 111	Schipol	N-101–N-111
F.6	One batch of 144	Schipol	N-201–N-144
F.4	One batch of 95	Gosselies	ID-1–ID-95
F.6	One batch of 93	Gosselies	IF-1–IF-93

952 from Kingston
278 from Baginton, Coventry
299 from Blackpool
255 from Schipol, the Netherlands
188 from Gosselies, Belgium
Total: 1,972 Hunters

APPENDIX III

RAF and FAA Units

Unit	Base	Mark	Dates
1 Sqn	Tangmere	F.5	Sept. '55–June '58 db 1 July '58
	Stradishall	F.6	2 July '58–Mar. '60
	Waterbeach	FGA.9	Jan. '60
	West Raynham		13 Aug. '63
	Wittering		18 July '69
2 Sqn	Jever	FR.10	Mar. '61
	Gutersloh	FR.10	9 Sept. '61. db 31 Mar. '71
3 Sqn	Geilenkirchen	F.4	May '56 db 15 June '57
IV Sqn	Jever	F.4	July '55–Feb. '57
		F.6	Feb. '57–Dec. '60. db 30 Dec. '60
8 Sqn	Khormaksar	FGA.9	Jan. '60
		FR.10	Apr. '61–May '63, Sept. '67–Dec. '71
	Bahrain		30 June '61 and Farwania
	Khormaksar		14 Oct. '61, db 21 Dec. '67
14 Sqn	Oldenburg	F.4	June '55–May '57
		F.6	Apr. '57
	Ahlhorn		26 Sept. '57
	Gutersloh		15 Sept. '58
	Jever		16 Mar. '61
	Gutersloh		6 Sept. '61. db 17 Dec. '62
19 Sqn	Church Fenton	F.6	Oct. '56
	Leconfield		29 June '59–Feb. '63
20 Sqn	Oldenburg	F.4	Nov. '55–June '57
		F.6	May '57
	Ahlhorn		23 Sept. '57
	Gutersloh		30 Aug. '58 db 30 Dec '60
	Tengah	FGA.9	1 Sept. '61 db 18 Feb. '70

26 Sqn	Oldenburg	F.4	June '55 db 10 Sept. '57
	Ahlhorn	F.6	7 June '58
	Gutersloh		8 Sept. '58 db 30 Dec. '60
28 Sqn	Kai Tak	FGA.9	May '62 db 2 Jan. '67
34 Sqn	Tangmere	F.5	Oct. '55 db 15 Jan. '58
41 Sqn	Biggin Hill	F.5	June '55 db 31 Jan '58
43 Sqn	Leuchars	F.1	July '54–Nov. '56
		F.4	Feb. '56–July '58
		F.6	Nov. '56–Dec. '56, Jan. '58–July '60
		FGA.9	May '60–Oct. '67
	Nicosia		21 June '61
	Khormaksar		1 Mar. '63 db 7 Nov. '67
45 Sqn	West Raynham	FGA.9	1 Aug. '72
	Wittering		29 Sept. '72 db 26 July '76
54 Sqn	Odiham	F.1	Feb. '55–Sept. '55
		F.4	Sept. '55–Jan. '57
		F.6	Sept. '55–Jan. '57
	Stradishall		17 July '59
		FGA.9	Mar. '60–Sept. '69
	Waterbeach		23 Nov. '61
	West Raynham		14 Aug. '63
	Coningsby		1 Sept. '69 to Phantoms
56 Sqn	Waterbeach	F.5	May '55–Nov. '58
		F.6	Nov. '58–Jan. '61
	Wattisham		10 July '59
58 Sqn	Wittering	FGA.9	1 Aug. '73–26 July '76 db
63 Sqn	Waterbeach	F.6	Nov. '56–db 30 Oct. '58
65 Sqn	Duxford	F.6	Nov. '56–db 31 Mar. '61
66 Sqn	Linton-on-Ouse	F.4	Mar. '56–Jan. '57
		F.6	Oct. '56–Sept. '60
	Acklington		14 Feb. '57 db 30 Sept. '60
67 Sqn	Brüggen	F.4	Jan. '56–31 May '57 db
71 Sqn	Brüggen	F.4	Apr. '56–31 May '57 db
74 Sqn	Horsham St Faith	F.4	Mar. '57–Jan. '58
		F.6	Nov. '57–Nov. '60
	Coltishall		8 June '59 to Lightnings
92 Sqn	Linton-on-Ouse	F.4	Apr. '56–Mar. '57
	Middleton St George		1 Mar. '57
		F.6	Mar. '57–Apr. '63
	Thornaby		30 Sept. '57
	Middleton St George		1 Oct. '58

	Leconfield		22 May '61 to Lightnings Apr. '63
93 Sqn	Jever	F.4	Jan. '56–Mar. '57
		F.6	Mar. '57–30 Dec. '60 db
98 Sqn	Jever	F.4	19 Apr. '55–25 July '57 db
111 Sqn	North Weald	F.4	June '55–Nov. '56
		F.6	Nov. '56–Aug. '61
	North Luffenham		19 Feb. '58
	Wattisham		18 June '58
112 Sqn	Brüggen	F.4	Apr. '56–31 May '57 db
118 Sqn	Jever	F.4	6 May '55–22 Aug. '57 db
130 Sqn	Brüggen	F.4	Apr. '56–31 May '57 db
208 Sqn	Nicosia	F.6	1 Mar. '58–31 Mar. '59 db
	Stradishall	FGA.9	29 Mar. '60–Sept. '71
	Eastleigh		3 June '60
	Bahrain & Farwania		30 June '61
	Khormaksar		15 Nov. '61
	Eastleigh		30 Nov. '61
	Khormaksar		9 Dec '61
	Muharraq		8 June '64–10 Sept. '71 db
222 Sqn	Leuchars	F.1	Dec. '54–Aug. '56
		F.4	Aug. '56–1 Nov. '57 db
234 Sqn	Geilenkirchen	F.4	May '56–15 July '57 db
245 Sqn	Stradishall	F.4	Apr. '57–30 June '57 db
247 Sqn	Odiham	F.4	May '55–Mar. '57
		F.6	Mar. '57–31 Dec. '57 db
257 Sqn	Wattisham	F.2	Sept. '54–Mar. '57
	Wymeswold		10 June '56
	Wattisham		15 Jan. '57–31 Mar. '57 db
263 Sqn	Wattisham	F.2	Feb. '55–Aug. '56
		F.5	May '55–Aug. '56
	Wymeswold		10 June '56
		F.6	Aug. '56–July '58
	Wattisham		15 Jan. '57
	Stradishall		30 Aug. '57–2 July '58 db
12 Sqn	Honington	F.6	Feb. '80–'84
	Lossiemouth	F.6	4 Aug. '80
15 Sqn	Laarbruch	F.6	Feb. '80, absorbed by 16 Sqn 1 July '83
16 Sqn	Laarbruch	F.6	Feb. '80, db 29 Feb. '84
216 Sqn	Honington	F.6	Feb. '80
	Lossiemouth		4 July '80, absorbed by 12 Sqn 4 Aug. '80

229 OCU	Chivenor	F.1, F.4, F.6/6A, T.7, FGA.9, FR.10	1955–2 Sept. '74. 234 Sqn Nov. '58, 145 Sqn Nov. '58–1 June '63, 63 Sqn 1 June '63, 79 Sqn Jan '67
233 OCU	Pembrey	F.1	1956–1 Sept. '57 db
1 TWU	Brawdy	F6/6A, FGA.9, T.7	2 Sept. '74 with 63, 79 & 234 Sqn
	Chivenor		db 31 Aug. '92
2 TWU	Lossiemouth	T.7, FGA.9	31 July '78–1 Apr. '81 db. 63 & 151 Sqn
	Chivenor	T.7, FGA.9	1 Apr. '81–1 Apr. '92 as 7 FTS
HCU	Wittering	FGA.9	1 Jan. '69–'70
1417 Flt	Khormaksar	FR.10	Mar. '63–'67
4 FTS	Valley	F.6, T.7	1967–*c*. '74
738 NAS	Lossiemouth	GA.11, T.8	June '62–May '70
	Brawdy		1 Jan. '64–8. May '70 db
759 NAS	Brawdy	T.8	July '63–24 Dec. '69 db
764 NAS	Lossiemouth	T.8	Dec. '58–27 July '72 db
		GA.11 & PR.11	July '62–27 July '72 db
899 NAS	Yeovilton	T.8M	Aug. '81–'82

APPENDIX IV

Specifications

F.1

Powerplant:	One R-R Avon Mk 113 rated at 7,500 lb thrust
Dimensions:	Span: 33 feet 8 inches; length: 45 feet 10.5 inches; height: 13 feet 2 inches; wing area 340 sq. feet
Weights:	12,128 lb empty, 16,200 lb loaded
Performance:	Max speed at sea level 610 kts, M 0.93 at 36,000 feet, service ceiling 48,500 feet
Fuel capacity:	334 gal.
Armament:	Four 30-mm Aden cannons in detachable pack under cockpit

F.2

Powerplant:	One A-S Sapphire Mk 101 rated at 8,000 lb thrust
Dimensions:	As for F.1
Weights:	As for F.1
Performance:	Max speed at sea level 612 kts, M 0.94 at 36,000 feet, service ceiling 50,000 feet
Fuel capacity:	314 gal.
Armament:	As for F.1

F.4

Powerplant:	One R-R Avon Mk 113, 115, 119, 120, 121 or 122 rated at 7,500–8,000 lb thrust
Dimensions:	As for F.1
Weights:	12,543 lb empty, 17,100 lb loaded
Performance:	Max speed at sea level 610 kts, M 0.94 at 36,000 feet, service ceiling 50,000 feet
Fuel capacity:	414 gal. + additional capacity in 400-gal. underwing tanks
Armament:	Four 30-mm Aden cannons, plus selection of underwing stores, including 2-inch rockets, 500-lb or 1,000-lb bombs, 3-inch RP, 100-gal. napalm tanks

F.5

Powerplant:	As for F.2
Dimensions:	As for F.2
Weights:	As for F.4
Performance:	As for F.2
Fuel capacity:	388 gal. + additional in 400-gal. underwing tanks
Armament:	As for F.4

F.6

Powerplant:	One R-R Avon Mk 203/207 rated at 10.000 lb thrust
Dimensions:	As for F.1 except wing area increased to 349 sq. feet with l/e extensions
Weights:	12,760 lb empty, 17,750 lb loaded
Performance:	Max speed at sea level 620 kts, M 0.95 at 36,000 feet, service ceiling 48,900 feet
Fuel capacity:	390 gal. + additional in 600-gal. underwing tanks
Armament:	As for F.4

T.7/8

Powerplant:	As for F.4 except for T.66 as for F.6
Dimensions:	As for F.1 except for length 48 feet 10.5 inches
Weights:	13,360 lb empty (13,580 lb Mk 66), 17,200 lb loaded (17,420 lb Mk 66)
Performance:	Max speed 603 kts at sea level, M 0.92 at 36,000 feet (608 kts and M 0.93 Mk 66), service ceiling 47,000 feet (48,900 feet Mk 66)
Fuel capacity:	414 gal. + 400 gal. in underwing tanks. (390 gal. + 660 in Mk 66)
Armament:	One 30-mm Aden cannon under stbd side of nose (two Aden guns under nose of Mk 66)

FGA.9

Powerplant:	As for F.6
Dimensions:	As for F.6
Weights:	13,010 lb empty, 18,000 lb loaded
Performance:	As for F.6
Fuel capacity:	As for F.6
Armament:	As for F.6

FR.10

Powerplant:	As for F.6
Dimensions:	As for F.1 apart from length 46 feet 1 inches
Weights:	13,100 lb empty, 18,090 lb loaded
Performance:	As for F.6
Fuel capacity:	As for F.6
Armament:	As for FGA.9 plus three nose mounted cameras

GA.11

All data the same as F.4 except for gun armament deleted and provision for rocket batteries on underwing pylons.